T0354607

Remember When....

BRYAN P. CHRYSLER

authorHOUSE®

AuthorHouse™
1663 Liberty Drive
Bloomington, IN 47403
www.authorhouse.com
Phone: 1-800-839-8640

Names of some of the persons in this book have been changed to protect
their privacy. I have tried to re-create the story authentically, only
fictionalizing when my memory failed. I would like to thank my
editors, Lynn Kelly and Penny Chrysler for their outstanding job.

First published by AuthorHouse 11/23/2011

ISBN: 978-1-4670-6646-4 (sc)
ISBN: 978-1-4670-7204-5 (e)

Library of Congress Control Number: 2011919161

Printed in the United States of America

Any people depicted in stock imagery provided by Thinkstock are models,
and such images are being used for illustrative purposes only.
Certain stock imagery © Thinkstock.

This book is printed on acid-free paper.

Dedicated to my wife,
Penny

And
The Class of 1966

Chapter 1
All is Well

I ran through the kitchen and hit the screen door without slowing down, heading towards my second-hand Huffy lying on its side in the dew leaden grass. The late spring sun was unusually warm this June morning. School had been out for several weeks, long enough to form a group of ornery, but well meaning boys that lived on the north-end. I righted my well used bicycle, swung my leg over the bar and put all my forces on the right peddle turning towards my friend Gaiter's. His house was across the street. There never was enough traffic to warrant looking both ways. We would listen for the sound of an approaching vehicle and if it was far enough away we would hear it crossing the bridge's wooden planked surface at the bottom of Mule's Hill with a bam-bam, bam-bam of the tires thumping the uneven surface. Crossing Washington Street, I emitted a screech that sounded somewhat like a crow's call, but in fact, it was our secret call. Gaiter ran out of his house and raised his bicycle along with Billy, who lived on the same side of the street that I did, with one house between us. Gaiter and Billy answered the call with crow calls of their own. Meeting along the ditch, which bordered the street,

Billy asked, "What are we going to do?" I answered, one-half statement and one-half question, "Go up-town…." And off we rode down the middle of Washington Street.

In a minute we came to the "haunted house" on the corner of Ohio and Washington Streets. An old gingerbread one story dwelling, with little paint, setting on an overgrown lot not tended in years. As usual, we slowed down and pulled to the left side of Washington, hopefully to catch a glimpse of the lady that lived there. Ill-informed, we referred to her as "The Witch". Luck did not shine on us that day, nor had it in the days prior to that. It was said, one may see the yellowed window blind move out from the glass pane as she surveyed who was causing the disturbance in a world outside of hers. We were blessed with vivid imaginations. We claimed to see the blind move frequently and would exuberantly testify it was "The Witch". Sometimes one of us would get up the courage to pick up a stone and throw it hitting the side of the old house. But today, this wasn't the case. We each made a crow call or two and picked up speed moving to the center of the street. Riding in the center of the street was an act of defiance and one of the things that reinforced our companionship.

We rode within one block of Main Street and traffic in that area forced us to ride on the sidewalk. The block north of Main Street was busy. There was only one funeral home in town located close to the Post Office and the newspaper office. People came and went at the Post Office in the morning picking up their mail and a few depositing letters that would travel to far away unknown places. The funeral home was usually quiet in the morning as was the newspaper office on Mondays. It was another story on Wednesday. Wednesday was the day the paper 'came out' as we called it. There was a poster in the newspaper window. It was red, white, and black proclaiming the upcoming Agricultural Fair in July. We always liked the Daredevils on Saturday night, the last day of the fair. For several weeks after, we would make ramps and ride our bikes over them like the daredevils we saw perform those fantastic stunts.

During the hot July week we would wander up and down the Midway, mostly looking, but sometimes we would hear of a carnival booth where somebody won a marvelous prize and we would take some of our mowing and bottle money and try our luck. Pop bottles could be redeemed for two cents each, a great way to supplement our income. My best prize was a black rubber shrunken head attached to a black stick by a string. It had black marble eyes and black silky hair with a small silver ring through its nose. Dangling the strange looking black rubber orb over an un-expecting girls' shoulder was a great past-time. Although by Thursday, the fourth day of the fair, they were accustomed to the shrunken head prank because almost every boy had won one. Instead of being frightened they acted angry and would try to grab the head and break the black string or stick if they were fast, then stomping it in the talc like dust underfoot on the Midway.

We swerved left cutting the corner and stopped on the cement that took up an area used as an auto repair shop. It was an open outside area and on the north wall of the building was a small office. Gentlemen sat outside this door in the morning hours until the sun raised enough to make it uncomfortably warm. We didn't know what they did but we somehow realized we were not welcome in that circle. We sat at that corner for a short time. Finally Gaiter rode diagonally across the intersection and Billy and I were close behind. We went behind the Marathon Station

3

looking for discarded pop bottles and any new wrecked cars in the lot where Neal parked them. He owned an auto repair shop and towing business located behind the Martinsville State Bank, just south of Main Street. Gaiter was there first and picked up two pop bottles. One bottle had been used to dispense an oily substance and when he put it in his basket the remaining oil dripped on his front tire. This could make tight cornering difficult but Gaiter didn't seem to mind. All he needed was one more bottle and he could purchase a cold soft drink at Murph's. Murph's was an amazing place to hang out. Murph didn't seem to care how long you were there. The older boys sat behind the glassed cooler on boxes of unopened can goods smoking cigarettes and drinking pop. We were still a little too young to join them. Murph had a gum machine that looked like a rocket ship and dispensed larger than normal gum balls for one cent. The favorite gum machine, a one-center dispensed much smaller gum balls; but, lurking behind the machine's display glass was the strategically placed, coveted blacked striped blue gum balls. If you were very lucky the machine might dispense a black striped blue ball that could be traded in to Murph for five cents! This machine got the most action. We were unsuccessful in finding any more bottles so Gaiter decided to try his luck at the gum machine. He cashed in his two bottles and took his fortune and deposited one cent at a time into the chrome slot on the front of the machine. He turned the handle and heard a gum ball roll down the shoot and rest against the flapper door that he held closed with his left hand. For luck he repeated this with the three pennies remaining before allowing the door to open. Gaiter took a deep breath while we held ours and opened the chrome door. And there was a green gum ball, a red, a white and a blue one with black stripes!

Gaiter gave Murph the blue gum ball with black stripes. Murph pulled the worn leather thong that he used to open the cash register drawer because the release was broken. He handed a nickel to Gaiter. Gaiter took the red gum ball and let Billy and I have the green and white one. I was lucky because I grabbed first and got the green one. All of us chewed to the rhythm of the old cooler compressor running in the small back room and I asked, "What do you want to do now?" Billy and I looked at each other and turned to see a smile come across Gaiter's face as he looked at us. He suggested, take the five cents and purchase two cigarettes and reinvest in the gum machine the one remaining penny. We nodded approval and Gaiter turned to Murph and said, "Give me two Camels." Murph didn't hesitate and handed him two Camels and a penny from the old cash register which Billy quickly inserted into the machine. He got a black gum ball which he threw in his mouth. I asked Gaiter if he had any matches. He smiled showing teeth stained by the black gum ball. A smile from Gaiter meant yes.

Gaiter said, "I'm not in the mood to smoke, let's find the Old Lawyer," an elderly man, who it was said, was a retired Chicago lawyer. Each fair-weather day he dressed in a three piece suit, very smart had it been thirty years earlier. We called him "The Lawyer". The lawyer would walk down Main Street, especially in front of the two restaurants, seeking discarded cigarette or cigar butts. When he would see one, he would begin his ritual to retrieve the butt, which he then would use, to satisfy his need for nicotine. The Lawyer would spot a butt on the sidewalk, stop, and take a book of matches from his vest pocket. He would hang his cane on his left arm and unfold the book of matches. Then, as if magic, he would drop the matches next to the spent butt. In one swipe of his nimble fingers, the lawyer would pick up his matches with the butt and hold it as if it were a nugget of gold. He would light his find and continue his walk with a look of contentment on his face, as a laborer after a days work.

This is where we came in. Murph kept an apparatus that dispensed string from a large spool hanging close above the counter. We asked him for a piece which he gave us somewhat reluctantly. We left our bikes leaning on the store front window ledge and ran back to Main Street looking for the lawyer. There he was walking slowly between the two restaurants. Getting close to the Playhouse Café, we hoped he would turn around and head back toward the Highway Café. We ran across Main Street hiding between two parked cars close to the center, between the restaurants. Gaiter carefully took one of the cigarettes and tied on a length of the string. We looked down the sidewalk and here came the lawyer. Gaiter discretely threw the new cigarette onto the walk in front of the first car to the left of our hiding place. As we peeked around and under the car, the lawyer began his ritual. As soon as the book of matches landed next to the cigarette, Gaiter pulled the weed about a foot toward us. Out of reach, the lawyer picked up the matches, grasped his cane and took a step and a half toward us. He once again hung his cane on his left arm and removed the book of matches from his vest pocket. Then after opening the book of matches he dropped them next to the trophy he longed for. Gaiter again pulled the cigarette towards us but maybe a little too much because it was between the cars, in front of our hiding place. We glanced at each other hoping someone had a plan, but it was too late because the old lawyer was standing on the sidewalk between the two cars looking directly at us. In unison, we broke into a run across Main Street, to the safety of the north sidewalk.

But, to our dismay, there was the old Lawyer happily admiring his new treasure that we mistakenly left behind! We walked to Murph's, got our bikes, and started back the half block to Main Street then turned right.

We rode past the Zenith store, the bakery, and stopped at Mauks Drug Store. Billy was first to the heavy door and opened it easily. We didn't run but it seemed we were in a hurry. Billy and I went to the cigar lighter. A wooden box sat on top of the tobacco counter with two brass upright pieces, one with a wick running threw it with only a small black lump of it showing, and another piece that had a wire affixed to its end. That piece was hinged. One would grasp a small handle and pull the second piece and the wire would come close to the first. This is when a big electric spark would dance from the wire to the wick and the wick would burst into flame. Billy and I took turns pulling the top wire electrode across the wick lighting it. It was great fun but we had to keep alert for the druggist. He never asked us to leave and we wanted to keep it that way. We were intent on not wearing out our welcome and spoil our chance to make the spark! The cigar lighter was a grand experience to return to again and again, when the occasion presented itself. We never tired of sparking the thing and watching the yellow flame.

Gaiter went to the magazine rack looking at the current issue of Boys Life as a decoy. The items of interest were the detective magazines that could be found high on the rear of the display rack positioned against the wall, out of reach for young gentleman. Billy and I joined Gaiter and on tip toes, reached over the three or four neatly arranged rows of magazines and lifted our selections up just enough to look at the picture of a woman on the front cover. We still thought girls were something to throw rocks at, but we also were old enough to be intrigued, although not fully understanding why. Besides it would be a breach of comradeship if one of us would leave the pack because of a girl, unless it was to cause her physical harm or embarrassment. This would change in time.

Gaiter noticed the clerk watching us from the counter which was right of the magazine rack. The good thing was, she couldn't see what magazines we were looking at from her viewpoint. He said, "Let's get out of here!" We both agreed with Gaiter, possibly in fear of being approached by the clerk and the embarrassment of a reprimand from a woman for looking at girly pictures. We left the drug store hurriedly once again heading west on Main Street.

Passing the Ross Shop and Sinclair Implements, an Allis Chalmers dealership, we pulled up at the Five and Ten Cent Store called Margie's. Margie's husband, Jerry, usually waited on the young male cliental. Margie's store had a wonderful smell. Upon entering, you were surrounded by an odor sweet to the senses, but unlike any other. It seeped from the candy display just left of the entry door. There were at least twelve, maybe more, glass divisions containing some of the best candy in town. It was the only place in town where you could purchase candy by the pound. Every known candy was just out of reach behind a thick pane of plate glass. If Jerry noticed someone in front of the candy case he would move behind the display and remove a white paper sack from a shelf below, snapping open the small bag by flicking it with a fast movement of his wrist. He would pick up a shiny metal scoop and make eye contact with the customer. With a smile Jerry would say, "What would you like today?" A master marketing move only used by the best businessmen. I noticed Jerry coming towards the candy counter and pulled at Billy's tee-shirt sleeve indicating that we should leave the candy display to avoid embarrassment. We had no money and only one Camel that Gaiter kept carefully lodged in a hole enlarged on his bicycle's right handgrip. It was in his right grip simply because he didn't have a left one. I made a move to the right in the narrow store looking forward to the plastic models that were located down one of the two isles close to the rear of the store. To my surprise, Gaiter and Billy headed out the door, I turned and followed. Once past the door while picking up my bicycle I said, "Those chocolate turtles sure looked good!" Gaiter said, "Yah they did, but all we have is this Camel." Billy suggested, "Let's smoke it! Do you guys have any matches?" He had forgotten that Gaiter had a book that he didn't admit he had.

We took off riding west; past the auto repair shop, noticing the men had left their bench because the late morning sun made their perch uncomfortable. Sort of looking for traffic, we raced across Washington Street to the next open concrete lot where Dick Lake operated the F/S Filling Station. Dick specialized in tires. He and his helper Don would play catch on slow days. The pneumatic car lift had a shed roof over it, somewhat of an improvement over their neighbor on the opposite side of the street. Dick was well respected in the community and surrounding areas. He functioned as an MC at our fair and adjoining county's fairs. If an event required an MC, Dick would do the job and do it skillfully! He excelled announcing local sporting events and would say, "Here come the Big Blue!" when the game was about to start or just before crucial plays on the football field. Our high school teams were called the Blue Streaks. We waved at Dick and Don as Don's glove popped, from one of his bosses' fast balls.

We made our way to a good place to have a smoke. An

area between the American Legion building and Library that was much lower than the surrounding area. The Legion had a walkway with a few steps that lead to a door opening into a lower level called the basement. This door was used in the late afternoon by local men. Our town was dry but we would see them sipping beer in the late afternoon because sometimes the door would be left open. But in the late morning it was usually deserted making it a perfect hiding place to conduct our experimental trials in mastering the use of tobacco. Gaiter removed the Camel cigarette from his right hand grip and we followed him down the concrete entryway. Sitting on the cool steps, Gaiter lit a match and held it to the end of the cigarette held between his lips and drew in a breath of air. Coughing with a glassy-eyed look, he handed the smoke to me and I took a puff. After a drag and considerable effort not to cough, I handed the cigarette to Billy. He did well. Billy took a long drag and exhaled like a pro. It seemed he had more practice than Gaiter or me. We passed the smoke around a few times until it was mostly spent. Billy took the last drag, partly because he wanted to and partly because Gaiter and I had had more than we wanted. In fact we all were a little dizzy. It was getting close to lunch time and the fresh air on our faces during the short bicycle ride to the north side of town was just what we needed before lunch. Off we went pedaling north on Washington Street.

We split the formation apart. I turned into the yard as Gaiter and Billy kept going north the short distance to their homes. Nothing was said because it was customary to meet at Gaiter's after lunch. I rode hard towards the back door and locked the brake and the rear wheel slid easily. I shifted my weight and the rear wheel came around as I let the bicycle drop to the ground close to the steps. I ran up the steps and opened the screen door, entered into the back room, then the kitchen before I heard the screen door slam shut.

"Hi Mom," I said as she gave me the same look that she always gave me when I let the screen door slam shut, then she smiled and said, "Lunch is ready but please go wash your hands." All was well.

Chapter 2
The Lake

I ate as fast as I could. I have been accused of not chewing my food on numerous occasions. It didn't take long to eat a baloney sandwich and drink a glass of milk. Besides, I wanted to be the first guy back out and let loose with a crow call. I had a tinge of guilt about not talking much to Mom but I didn't want her to smell the cigarette smoke on my breath. She said something about where I had been and what I was planning for the afternoon. Not chewing my food, leaving those questions unanswered, I responded with a smile that exposed Wonder Bread stuck between my teeth. I guess she was happy knowing that it "Helped to Build Strong Bodies 12 Different Ways."

I ran through the back room out to my Huffy and took off towards Gaiter's. I dropped down into the ditch, made two more revolutions of the pedals, and crossed the ditch on Gaiter's side of the street. Wasting no time, I stopped, cupped both hands in front of my mouth, and made two crow calls. Seeing nor hearing nothing, I made a third call just as I saw the back door crack open. Gaiter came out; I dropped my bike and followed him to the "Barn". The barn was a modern structure for a barn. It had one room finished which was once used as a hobby room or something and a pull-down ladder in the ceiling that opened to the loft. The loft had a secondary entrance or escape route. This was a door that swung out from the loft floor just big enough to enter or exit comfortably. Several boards were removed from the side of the barn below the loft door providing hand and foot holds so we could easily come and go.

Hoss and his bicycle

Gaiter didn't say anything as we entered the barn. I figured his mother scolded him for something. We set Indian style on the cement floor that had traces of green paint. I picked up a wire that looked like it once was part of a coat hanger and slowly pecked it on the floor in front of my knees. After some hope that Gaiter would say something I broke the ice by saying the first thing that came to my mind. "Let's go to the lake..." Gaiter half-way smiled and softly said, "OK."

We went out to our bikes and I made three or four

more crow calls hoping to see Billy come out of his house across the street. The other side of the street looked like a ghost town. It was the quiet time of the day, twenty past noon. Billy didn't answer the call so that meant he either was in trouble or his mom was going to make him take a nap. Either possibility wasn't good. We were too old to be taking naps and Billy didn't do anything that we knew of. Maybe his mother smelled smoke on his breath! I hope not because this could get back to my mom.

My thoughts quickly left Billy's situation and I became aware that Gaiter had pushed off and crossed the ditch heading north towards Mule Hill. I caught up with him at the top of the hill and it was a race down to the bridge. It was important to get there first. The first rider could select the right side plank which was much smoother than the warped left plank. The planks were laid on oak timbers positioned in the opposite direction with a considerable gap between them. Missing or driving off the planks always concerned us because we almost always made the crossing at high speed. I know of no one who may have had a wreck on the bridge, but if someone did, they wouldn't brag about it. Gaiter made it first and I braked hard lining up behind him. After the successful crossing we came to the highway, US 40, a heavily traveled route. We both came to a stop because this was one place where we would stop, look, and listen!

We set there for a long time, it seemed, before an opening in the traffic appeared. Taking off as fast as we could, we crossed US 40 and started up the hill, leading to Gaiter's grandparent's house. They owned the foundry, a large business for our town of less than 1200 people. The foundry made wheel weights for farm tractors and other weights for industry. They also owned the lake. It was a medium-sized lake that had more than enough exciting things to keep us occupied until late afternoon.

Approaching the house, Gaiter turned in the saddle and gave me a signal to be quiet by pressing his finger to his lips. Gaiter didn't get along well with his grandmother and wasn't close to his grandfather although I thought he wanted to be. I do not ever remember his grandfather speaking to him, nor Gaiter speaking to him either!

We made it past the house without being noticed, as far as we knew. There had been times that the dreaded red pick-up, Gaiter's grandfathers', would come down the road unnoticed until it was crossing the dam and by then it was too late to conceal any thing we wanted to conceal. He would never say anything, just give us a look. I don't think he was a mean man or unreasonable, he represented authority which made him an adversary. Once we received the look, we knew Gaiter's grandmother would have words with his mother. Gaiter's mother was an understanding woman and usually little would happen, other than a reprimand that was quickly forgotten. We continued down the road which was asphalt. The grounds surrounding the lake were kept very well as the amenities on or near the lake itself.

The first area we approached was what we called the "Baby Pool". A concrete area about twelve by sixteen feet and three feet deep with a roof built over the concrete enclosure. A large round handle was located on the left side of the road in the water. This was a valve used to release water into the baby pool from the lake. A good sized steel plug was used to place into the big drain pipe at the bottom of the pool to retain water. It normally was kept open, to act as a spillway after a rain. Actually, I think this was meant to be a baptistery, but we never saw anything like that happen.

We rode past the baby pool and up a small grade to the top of the dam. Crossing the long dam, we entered the trees on the east side of the lake. This large area contained a picnic area with tables and a large brick fireplace that sat on a concrete pad. In the past, Gaiter's grandparents would instruct the groundskeeper to keep a supply of fire wood close to the fireplace. This practice was halted. On more than one occasion we built a fire in the fireplace and fed it like a steam locomotive fireman, pulling a long train up a steep grade. The only thing that stopped our train was either we used up the supply of wood, or saw the red pick-up approaching.

It wasn't a very windy day so I suggested to Gaiter that we take the row boat out. I was much more of a "lake" person than Gaiter. Maybe it was because of possible unforeseen chastisement that could come his way for not behaving like a well-mannered young gentleman that dampened his enthusiasm. Regardless, Gaiter rarely took out his troubles on the rest of us. He gave a look that someone outside of our gang could interpret as no, but I knew he was game. We made our way to the boat house. A structure that was built on pilings that extended out into the water. At one time it didn't have a floor and a boat could be parked inside out of the unpredictable Illinois weather. Sometime in the past a floor had been installed and now it was used as a dressing room for swimmers and a storage place for Gaiter's granddad's fishing gear. It was well maintained as was the large deck that also extended out into the water. It had a picket fence surrounding the deck floor, and a gate that faced the open expanse of the lake. Next to the gate, which usually was open, was a metal ladder, extending down into the water. Everything was painted white. Between the boat house and deck there was an area of partially enclosed water with a passageway open to the west. The shallow bottom was covered with imported sand. This was where the row boat was kept. The distance from the concrete walk, also used as a retaining wall, and the water was more than two feet which made it necessary for me to sit down on the edge and place my feet on the row boat seat. While doing so I said, "Come on Gaiter!"

Chapter 3
The Frog

After Gaiter got positioned, I untied the boat and moved it out of the little enclosed area onto the main body of water. I grasped the heavy oars and pushed down on the handle ends lifting the paddle ends up and over the side of the boat then allowing them to enter the water. I paddled north around the swimming deck and toward the bank. I had just maneuvered the boat somewhat parallel with the bank when I bumped an old stump half in and half out of the water with an oar. It made a thump. Immediately we both heard a second thump and Gaiter lifted his feet. I looked at his face to see an open mouth and wide eyed sailor. Gaiter was pointing at surely the biggest bull frog in East Central Illinois! I loudly said, "Man, I want that one!"

I quickly looked around for anything to keep the bull frog from jumping out of the boat and found nothing but a cup or two of water in the bottom. I asked Gaiter if he could think of anything and he said, "I don't want the thing!" I couldn't let a prize like that get away, so I pulled my tee-shirt over my head and quickly threw it over the bull frog. The frog jumped just as the tee-shirt landed on him and I'm sure he was large enough to jump into the water tee-shirt and all, but as luck would have it, he hit the oar blinded by his tee-shirt cape. The giant bull frog fell into the bottom of the boat, allowing just enough time to grab him!

I held him down and carefully wrapped the tee-shirt around his large body being extra careful to incapacitate his powerful legs. I asked Gaiter to hold him down which he did with his feet until we got the row boat back between the boat house and dock. I took the weathered, white cotton rope that was tied to the bow of the boat and looped it twice through the white fence. I carefully placed my hands on the sides of Gaiter's tennis shoes and slipped down around the fat bull frog. Frog in hand, I ask Gaiter to steady the row boat and I used my forearms and elbows to crawl from the boat to the concrete sidewalk. It was hot on my forearms but, I had the frog!

We made it back to our bicycles and I inspected the tee-shirt to make sure the frog was secure. I made a few adjustments to the shirt so I could hold it like a sack because the frog was too large to hold with one hand. With great expectations, I pushed off on my Huffy with a somewhat less excited Gaiter close behind. I rode hard because I could only guess about the praise I expected to receive for capturing such a grand amphibian.

We approached Gaiter's grandparent's house silently and passed, turning south towards the highway at the bottom of the hill. We stopped, waiting for a chance to cross and I checked the semi-wet cotton bag hanging slightly below my right handgrip. Gaiter said, "Let's go!" I doubled checked, looking both ways and crossed slightly behind him. It wasn't because I didn't trust Gaiter; it just was a scary crossing even if you were a mighty amphibian wrangler.

Ahead was the bridge and Mule Hill. I crossed the bridge behind Gaiter. I planned on walking up the hill, pushing my bicycle anyway. Mule Hill was steep enough that it took hard pedaling which resulted in body language that could loosen my hold on the tee-shirt. Gaiter was standing in front of his house as the giant bull frog and I topped the hill. He raised his hand and I cocked my chin to signify that we would meet later. I checked the tee-shirt again as I re-mounted my Huffy and rode the short distance home.

Chapter 4
My Brother

Arriving in our back yard I looked across the neighbor's yard to see if Billy was out. I didn't see him so I let out a crow call. It was hot and I was tired, so the call wasn't very loud. I had a feeling that Billy had been confined for the day anyway. I stepped over the crossbar and let my bike gently to the ground. Not because I thought about protecting my Huffy but protecting my giant bull frog. I ran over to the well pump and pumped it about four times until I felt the weight of the water rising in the pipe. After a few more pumps water flowed from the spicket. I held the frog in it's tee-shirt under the flowing water. The tee-shirt was soaked good and I wondered what to do with the frog. My brother's red Radio Flyer was next to the big maple tree so I turned it over and carefully slipped the wet package under the wagon.

I needed to come up with a suitable home for the frog. I thought maybe the garage had something I could use. Half running, half walking, I went into the garage through the side door. It was dark inside; my eyes would take time to adjust. Standing by the door, being careful not to look behind at the bright light outside, I surveyed

what I could see and speculated about what I couldn't
see. Finally my eyes became accustomed to the gray light
inside the garage and I spotted an old wash boiler that
was blackened with age. Time had turned the copper tub
a dark gray-black color. I grabbed one of the handles and
gave it a few jerks to pull it out of its cluttered hiding
place. Several unknown items fell into a pile where the tub
was setting and tumbled out onto the floor. I dragged the
wash boiler towards the door while looking for something
I could use for the top of the new home for the frog.
Then, as magic, I saw the perfect thing. An old window
screen was leaning on the wall next to the door. I pulled
it straight up knocking a mortar trowel from its resting
place lodged behind a wall stud. It struck the screen near
the bottom. The point of the trowel hit the screen wire
at just the right angle tearing a three inch slit in the
rusty wire. I pulled the trowel from the screen and threw
it into the pile where the wash tub once was. It rattled
around before finding a resting place. I made it out the
door with the wash tub leaving the screen set just inside.
I pulled the wash tub over by the well pump and saw my
younger brother walking out of the weeds that took over
our garden.

My brother's name was Anson. Anson was six years
younger than me. Dad and I called him Andy but Mother
always called him Anson. He continued in my direction
just as I positioned the tub close to the wet lump of a
tee-shirt that I removed from under the wagon. I wanted
it ready. Andy came to a halt when he saw the tee-shirt,
knowing by its shape, something was in it and it may be
alive!

I loved my brother but it seemed he was always at
the right place at the right time to receive whatever
the torment of the day was. Andy was a great person

to test pranks or whatever on. He was too small to be a real physical threat to me and could be lured into a compromising situation rather easily. Andy asked in an uncertain voice, "What's in the rag?" I said, "Andy, that's not a rag, that's my tee-shirt." He said, "Mom's going to be mad." By that time the tee-shirt had seen its better days. It looked like an old rag that had been lying on the floor board of a farm truck for six months. "Andy, come here, see what I got," I said. He kept at a safe distance and said, "Show me Hoss." Now my real name wasn't Hoss, it was Bryan, but I liked Hoss. That was what my dad called me when he was proud or amused. I said, "You need to come closer."

Freckles, Anson, Darlene, and Hoss

Andy stood there, holding his ground. I shrugged my shoulders and shook my head portraying disbelief, disbelief that anyone would not want to get a really close look at the biggest bull frog I had ever seen. Andy had been conditioned in his short life to be very cautious of what I may or may not have. I went back to the garage and retrieved the old screen and on the way back said to Andy, "Come take a look," with a fake smile. Andy looked at me and then his attention would be redirected on the lump wrapped in the tee-shirt laying on the ground next to the old boiler tub, then back at me. He was trying to detect the slightest indication that I was about to launch an assault of some kind. I gave Andy a fake smile of concern and kindness and said, "Andy, I'm not going to do anything, come on and look." He looked embarrassed and that was what I wanted, knowing I had my foot in the door.

Just then the frog moved a move the tee-shirt did not conceal. Andy caught a glimpse and backed up three steps. It was going to be more difficult than I expected. He raised his voice to a nasal whimper and said, "Hoss, what do you have in there?"

I knew Andy was much more leery now and I needed to give him some space if I was going to succeed, in giving him his daily scare. I needed something to place in the bottom of the wash boiler for the frog to set on so I got up and walked toward the garden of weeds. I knew Dad had stacked a few bricks along its edge. Bricks would be just the thing for the frog to rest on. I walked along the edge of the garden, dragging my feet in the weeds to find the bricks. It was difficult going. The weeds, intertwined with tomato vines, made walking through this jungle almost impossible, especially dragging one's feet. It was hot in those weeds but I did find three bricks and a mother load of chiggers. The latter became evident late that night.

I placed the three bricks in the bottom of the old boiler and ran back to the garden where I pulled an arm load of weeds to take the place of moss in the bull frog's new home. Andy watched from a distance as I carefully placed the weeds around the bricks lying in the bottom of the copper boiler. Then I moved the boiler under the well pump and with a squeak that could cause goose bumps to rise on your arms during the hottest afternoons, I pumped the handle a few times, the squeak changing pitch under its load of water. I filled the tub with water to the bottom of the bricks. I noticed Andy had stepped forward the three steps he retreated earlier. Now I needed to entice him closer, close enough that I could grab his arm or at least close enough that I could give him an extra close surprise look at the bull frog.

"Andy, come here so I can show you this!" I said. He looked down at his feet and back at me. I smiled a reassuring smile and tried to act as relaxed as possible. Actually, I was as charged up as our tom cat Freckles was when I held him up to the clothesline post to hear the baby birds chirp after I made a little whistle. It was time to make the closing move. I said, "OK, I don't care if you see it or not." I drug the boiler over to the tee-shirt placed the screen next to it. Andy had taken another step closer. It was time! Like the strike of Freckles' paw I grabbed Andy's left arm and dragged him one and a half knee steps closer to the tee-shirt. He was thrashing violently trying to escape but I managed to hold his arm with one hand and pick up the bull frog in the tee-shirt in the other. I carefully positioned and repositioned the wet surprise. I finally brought the frog and rolled up tee-shirt to my lower chest to help control the frog who by that time was almost as concerned as Andy was. Like a surgeon working to save a life I maneuvered the frog from the tee-shirt. Andy, catching his first glimpse of the frog, was hysterical! I thrust the frog towards his face. I have never seen anyone more frightened than Andy was that day. He had realized his personal phobia with a little help from his big brother! His hidden strength came into play about then. You have heard of people performing extraordinary feats when in duress. Andy did! His eyes looked demonic! Like a bolt of lightning he became stronger than a teenager. With a twist and jerk of his left arm Andy was free and running towards the house crying wildly for Mother.

Shortly after I heard the screen door slam came the call that I was hoping not to hear, "Bryan!" I placed the bull frog in its new home and then answered in my best angelic voice, "Yah….." "You get into this house now!" Mom said. I reluctantly left my bull frog and started the walk towards the back screen door when I heard, "Hurry up!" I was close to the house when the screen door flew open. Mom allowed it to slam closed, against one of her policies. I knew she was angry, real angry! She grabbed my arm and her nails dug into my skin. "What did you do to your brother?" Mom said in anger. I said, "Accidentally a frog scared him…" That didn't go over very well. She sent me to my bedroom to wait for the arrival of my dad. The suspense of the wait was demanding but I had hopes that Dad would take pity on me and somehow realize that I was just trying to show Andy my frog. In fact I surely saved Andy from being attacked!

The longest forty-five minutes of my life passed as I laid on my bed looking out my bedroom window at the drive awaiting Dad's arrival. Down the street came Dad after his days work. It had been an unusually warm June day and I knew he wouldn't be in the mood to hear about Andy and me. Dad opened the door of his truck, stepped out, and turned to pick up his aluminum lunch pail and Stanley thermos that sat on the front seat. He was a tall man and he wore blue jeans with a matching shirt and a "steam fitter's hat." The hat had a short bill and was blue with large white poke-a-dots! That was the custom for welders.

Mother had Dad's coffee poured in his favorite cup by the time he sat his lunch pail and thermos down in front of the basement door. He sat at his usual place at the kitchen table and reached in his denim shirt pocket for his cigarettes. He started to tap the pack on his half closed fist of his other hand and before he could give them the customary four to five thumps, Andy ran to Mom and grabbed her apron. This was Andy's way to signal her to tell Dad about what I had done. Just before Mom opened her mouth Dad said, "Where's Hoss?" Mom said, as she turned toward dad with her hands on her hips and Andy hanging on her apron, "Dale, your oldest son almost scared the life out of Andy about an hour ago. I sent him to his room!" I could hear the conversation because there was a register in my bedroom floor, over the dining room located next to the kitchen. It was heavily used during times like these. There was a pause, and Dad, in his loud baritone voice said, "Bryan, come down here!" His voice was sobering, not because he could speak very loud, but because he called me Bryan and not Hoss. I slowly made it down the stairs and to the kitchen where I saw Mom standing there with the look on her face that said, now you are going to get it! Andy had a smirk on his face as he bent around Mom's leg to witness what was coming. Dad asked mom, "What did he do to Andy?" Mom replied with a cutting sharpness that only a loving mother could, "Your eldest son has a frog, or something in the back yard, which he threw in Anson's face!" Andy smiled and I shook my head in wonderment as if I didn't know what Mom was talking about. Dad said, "Martha, they are our sons." He threw his Camel pack onto the kitchen table as one would deal a playing card and turned in his chair bumping the table enough that coffee splashed over the rim of his cup. Some of the coffee entered into the neatly opened cigarette package and soaked into three before he could move them. Dad exclaimed, "Balls!" Balls was one of his favorite words when he was angry with himself or someone else. Sometimes it would be, "ah balls" if it was a lesser disappointment.

My Father at the kitchen table.

Dad looked at me, shook his head and said, "Hoss have you got a frog?" I said, "Yes." Dad asked, "And what did you do to Andy?" I said, "I accidentally let the frog scare him." Dad looked at Mom and then at Andy still hiding behind her then focused his attention back towards me. "You can forget TV tonight. I want you in your room after supper and your bath." Andy smiled and Mom looked pleased. Dad reached for the pack of cigarettes, forgetting about the coffee spill and started to pull one out and said it again with the extra Ah, "Ah Balls!" Actually I thought I got off the hook in good fashion and turned toward the doorway leading to the living room when Dad said, "Hoss, I want you to mow the yard tomorrow." I didn't want to hear that, nor did I enjoy the chiggers that night!

Chapter 5
The Drawing

Our summer vacation was about to end and we would be returning to school. The fair had come and past, I had nothing to show for all those hot afternoons, not even a shrunken head this year. I did get a shirt torn by Lee. He and Robert stopped Huck and I while we were walking down the Midway at the fair. Lee pulled me into a space under the grandstand between vender booths. He held me by the arms and told me they didn't like to be looked at. Huck and I did look their way and just after we made eye contact with them we turned to one another and shrugged our shoulders and laughed. Lee and Robert were two years older and Robert had his hair combed in a duck tail. They both were large for their age and were considered tough.

Huck was lucky. He almost always was. Lee grabbed me first and Robert stood by, leaving Huck on the Midway. I did my best, trying to act like I didn't know what they were talking about and Huck did his part by slightly opening his mouth, as surprised, and slowly shaking his head from side to side. Lee said, "We better not catch either one of you looking at us like that again." With a push, Lee said, "Get out of here and leave us alone!" I was very happy to follow his suggestion. Huck said, "They tore your shirt!" I did the only thing I could do, I looked over my shoulder to make sure those two older guys weren't looking and shrugged my shoulders, and we walked on.

It was Saturday. I hung around the house because Dad was home and I was hoping he would take me fishing. That was about my favorite pastime with Dad. But as luck would have it, the sewer was plugged up. It was a special delight for me to be the one to tell Dad the sewer was plugged. He would start off with an, "Ah balls!" As he ventured down the steps leading into the basement his vocabulary would become richer, especially if there was at least four inches of stinky gray water standing over the floor. This was about the time I knew to disappear.

The basement floor was dry this time so Dad turned around, on the stair steps, before reaching the basement floor. He went out the back door and into the garage with me following a respectable distance behind. He quickly stopped in the doorway and I was surprised because I ran into him. He turned to say, "What's wrong with you Hoss?" I knew by his look I should back off, way off! He went into the garage and I stayed just outside of the door. I heard him accidentally stumble over something and he exclaimed, "Damn!" The last straw, the thing that caused him to blow, was the pile of stuff halfway across the floor where I pulled the wash boiler from its storage place. It so happened, the sewer tape was in that pile. It usually was stored against the wall beside the wash boiler. Dad located the tape and jerked it three times before it became free. I turned away from the door because I didn't want to make eye contact. I knew his Saturday morning was going downhill from that moment on! I figured there wasn't any need to hang around him any more, so I turned away from the garage door to see Billy come out of his house.

I started running towards Billy's house while giving the crow call. He answered quickly with a crow call of his own. We met on the driveway in front of our neighbor's garage. Billy said, "Anything going on today, Hoss?" I said, "Nah....Nothing but the Drawing this afternoon. You goin'?" Billy said, "Yah, what time do you want to meet, about one?" I said, "OK.....I'll see you then."

I went back home and slipped into the house remembering not to let the screen door close with a slam. I walked through the back room to the open door at the top of the basement stairs. I heard the tinny, serpentine sound made by the sewer tape, as my dad wrestled it toward the clump of black roots, at about a distance of forty-five feet, that far away illusive root home. It sounded like dad was in a fight for his life with a giant slinky! I listened for a few new words but didn't hear any, just the well used ones that working the sewer tape generated.

In front of the TV

I went into the living room and turned the television on just in time. The screen was still gray although the small white dot had appeared and quickly vanished. I heard a few snaps and crackles then, "…..and Roy's wonder dog, Bullet!" The screen lit up, it was time for one of my favorite Saturday cowboy shows, *The Roy Rodgers Show.* I crawled over to the couch and took a pillow and moved back to my customary spot, on the floor, lying on my side in front of the TV.

The timing was good, because in a while, I heard Mom ask Dad how he was doing. I heard him say he was done and Mom said lunch was about ready. I turned off the TV after the song H*appy Trails* was over and made a dash to the kitchen. Andy was already in his chair. He looked like a hungry baby bird. I pulled my chair out hoping it would encourage mom to speed up, but it didn't. In fact, Mom ask, "Bryan, have you washed your hands?" She already knew my answer. I answered with a standard, "Ah Mom." I returned from the bathroom to see Dad emerge from the basement with the sewer tape neatly coiled in its retainer, dripping gray water across the kitchen and back room floor. Mom said, "Dale…." He looked down to see the water trail he had left on mom's recently mopped floor and said, "Balls!" Mom looked at us and said, "You boys wait until your Dad gets to the table." Dad came back through the house headed towards the bathroom while Mom re-mopped the floors. After a few minutes, Dad came into the kitchen, Mom sat down and we had lunch.

Riding my bike to Billy's I gave two crow calls and heard one from the initial tree. This was a large tree in front of Gaiter's neighbor's house with carvings of hearts, dates, and initials, thus it's name. The Fesonboch's lived north of Gaiter and the Winns' to the south. The tree was in Fesonboch's yard. I saw Gaiter's bike leaning against the trunk of the large tree. We needed to place a bicycle at the base of the tree and stand on its seat to reach the first limb. Gaiter was up the tree. I looked through the branches and couldn't see Gaiter so I gave out a crow call and soon received one in return. He was up there! I think he was in what he called the crow's nest. This was the highest point that Gaiter had ever climbed and he had climbed higher than anybody. I positioned myself on Gaiter's bicycle standing on the seat and reached for the first limb. Grabbing the limb with both hands, I swung my legs up and over the limb, then twisted my body so that I was lying on top and then sat up. About the time I got myself orientated, before I could say anything to Gaiter, I heard something I had never heard before. I realized it was Gaiter falling! He was cascading down, hitting the limbs on his way, and because of his momentum, could not maintain a secure hold. It seemed like it took forever. Gaiter didn't say anything on his way down, just a few short moans hitting large limbs during his descent. Then just as fast as it started, it finished, with him coming to rest on a large limb, only three above the one I was sitting on. He just laid there. I mustered up the courage to say, "Gaiter, are you ok?" It took him a few seconds to regain his composure. Gaiter, after a long pause answered in a weak voice, "Yeah, I think so." "Are you going to make it down ok?" I ask, and he said, "Yeah." I swung down holding onto the first limb feeling for the bicycle seat just below my tip toes. When I felt the seat, I let my self down the trunk of the tree and onto the ground. I was frightened because I wondered if Gaiter was really ok. I was thinking about going across the street and asking Billy to tell his mom when about then Gaiter was dangling from the first limb feeling, with his toes, for the bicycle seat. He slowly made it down beside me and I could tell he was hurting. His arms had several red scrapes and his right cheek had a place where the first layer of skin was peeled back about an inch and a half. I said to him, "Are you sure you are ok?" He said, "Yeah," again. I ask him if he was going to the drawing and he said no, walking towards his house next door. Gaiter went into hibernation for the rest of the day and wasn't seen until Monday.

I took Gaiter's bike to his house and laid it against the side of his house beneath his bedroom window. I got on my bike and went across the street to give Billy the news about Gaiter falling, giving a crow call as I was about across the street. Billy came out on his front porch by the time I reached the sidewalk, the one parallel with the street and the walk connecting the two steps extending from his porch, locked my brake and slid sideways to add a flair of intensity to the story I was about to tell. "Billy, Gaiter fell from the crows nest!" Billy said, "What?" "Yeah," I said, "All the way down to the third limb before he stopped!" "How bad did he get hurt?" Billy asks, with a look of concern. "Oh, he'll be ok," I said reassuringly. Billy shook his head as I did in return.

I thought it was about time to head towards town, so I ask Billy, "Are you ready to head out?" He said, "Yeah, but let me tell Mom." Billy ran to the front door and yelled through the screen, that he and I were going uptown. I heard Billy's mom say, "All right, be careful." We started the three and one half block ride towards town slowing down at the haunted house just enough to see if the blind was going to move. We both emitted crow calls. Billie and I speeded up darting from one side of the street to the other until we were at the corner of Washington and Main Street where we came to a stop and made eye contact with each other. Billy looked toward Hawk Eyes' and back at me. I gave him the nod that I was in favor of a visit to the pool hall. We rode across Main Street and dropped our bicycles in front of the Billiard Parlor.

We entered the open door to find Hawk Eye setting behind the glass counter which contained a box of Payday, a box of Snickers candy bars, and a few cubes of blue chalk used to apply to the ends of pool cues. And there was Huck! He signaled me to come over to the pinball machine. He pointed to the glass top which had a four inch crack on the right just over the ball plunger and the side slot that the shiny steel ball would go into, ending that round of play. When a ball would go down either side exit, the machine would reward the player one hundred points. The object of pinball was to get as many points as possible before the five balls were spent. Ten thousand points and the machine would reward a free game, and for each additional two hundred points after that, an additional game. Huck had a plan to insert his black hair comb through the crack in the glass and depress the triangle shaped wire that half protruded through a slit in the wood game surface. This would, hopefully, accumulate extra points without the loss of a ball. A nimble fingered guy could depress the trigger wire through the crack in the glass while the second guy played and blocked Hawk Eye's view. The pinball machine's bells and lights would cause quite a commotion while triggering and retriggering the wire located in the right hand ball exit slot. But, the real trouble was the "knock!" The pinball machine made this loud knocking noise, like a hammer striking a wood block when the machine rewarded a free game. It was easy after reaching ten thousand points to tap the exit wire two times, gaining two hundred points and a free game. We stopped at four games as Hawk Eye got up and looked our way. He sat down again when the machine quit ringing and knocking. We had four games to play! Huck pushed the metal button beside the coin return two times so he and I could both play.

The machine rang and lights flashed as it reset to zero. Huck backed away and slowly reached out his hand turning it over to expose his palm indicating for me to go first. We played four games, two each, although Huck stopped before flipping out his fifth and final ball. Huck turned to Billy and me and asked, "You guys want to "rack" up some more games?" I said, "Sure, can Billy play too?" Huck said, "Yeah, It will take up to four players." So Huck gave me the black hair comb and told Billy to watch Hawk Eye while we "racked" up some games. I carefully slipped the comb into the crack just in front of the triangle wire in the right exit slot so I could use a rocking motion to trip it. Huck pushed the chrome capped plunger that positioned a steel ball in front of the spring loaded plunger used to put the ball into play. Like a professional, Huck pulled the chrome knob towards himself gauging the length of the pull carefully using a scale printed on the machine. After readjusting the tension on the knob, Huck released the plunger sending the ball into play. It quickly rounded the top of the playing surface and bumped between the six slot bumpers several times before passing through, and then the bells started ringing and the lights flashing. It was now safe for me to start adding points. Hearing the excessive noise of the machine, Hawk Eye rose out of his chair behind the counter and started our way....just as a commotion started at the rear table. Two older guys were having words about something to do with the game of pea pool they were playing. Hawk Eye's attention was diverted to them so we decided to leave.

Huck joined Billy and I as we rode our bikes down the sidewalk zigzagging between ladies, gentlemen, and kids that came to town on Saturday to shop and for the Drawing. The drawing was held at two o'clock each Saturday by the Chamber of Commerce. If you were present in a business that was a member of the Chamber of Commerce and your name was written on a card, in a sealed envelope, opened at two o'clock you would win a cash credit that could be redeemed for merchandise. If the person was not present the cash credit would increase by five dollars. The drawing prize started at twenty five dollars. The drawing was a big event for our town.

We decided to go down to Murph's and loaf until two o'clock. I didn't have any money but I was in hope that Huck or Billy had some. Maybe they would share a Coke or something. The normal crowd was in Murph's, maybe six guys around our age in front of the well worn counter and the older guys in the aisle behind the cooler sitting on boxes, smoking. I was thirsty, but broke, and Huck or Billy didn't have any money either. We hung around watching the other young guys eat their five cent bags of potato chips and drink their Cokes waiting on Murph to open the drawing envelope that was stored between the side and the front of the cash register. The electric Doctor Pepper clock's second hand crossed it's most vertical position and Murph pulled the envelope from the side of the register. Usually I wouldn't pay much attention to the drawing but it took my mind from the thirst that I had that day. The others were not paying much attention either. Murph inserted his index finger under the envelope flap and tore it open, pulled the card out and read......my name! I could not believe it! I have never won anything before and now I had won the "Drawing!" I ask Murph how much it was for and he said twenty five dollars. "I had never had twenty five dollars in my life!" I said to Murph, "Can I spend some of it now?" Murph said, "Yes you can." After getting patted on the back by all the guys around the counter I made my way down the rear aisle to a black engineer boot and leg extended across the walkway. I looked into the face of Williams, the one who was blocking the aisle, for some kind of acknowledgement relating to my good fortune. All I received was a menacing stare and a, "What do you want kid?" I said nothing and made a quick retreat to the relative safety of the front counter. I said, "Murph, I'd like three Cokes and three bags of peanuts." I also said with an air of uncertainty to Murph, "Put that against my drawing winnings." Huck and Billy were just as happy as I was when Murph set the three bottles and three bags of peanuts on the old counter. Huck took a drink of Coke to lower the level so he could carefully empty his bag of nuts in the bottle. Billy and I just ate ours out of the bag between drinks of Coke. That was surely one, if not the best, Coke I had ever drunk!

We gave our empty bottles to Murph and went to our bikes that were leaning against the front of the store. Billy said, "Well we might as well head home." I said, "Ok, Huck are you going home or what?" Huck replied, "Well I best get home. I've got farther to go than you guys." Huck lived just north of town. So Billy and I left Murph's going east to Adams and Huck cut across town to the IGA which was located on the north east edge of town where he would ride down the hill and cross the dangerous US40. I rode fast leaving Billy behind. He didn't mind because he knew I wanted to tell Mom and Dad the news.

It didn't take long to reach home. I didn't slow down at the witch house either. I rode through our yard and dropped my Huffy just before I reached the steps and ran into the house allowing the back door to slam shut. Mom was waiting for me in the kitchen and Dad was sitting at the kitchen table drinking his favorite drink, black coffee. Mom was smiling, which was a surprise, because I knew I would get my usual scolding about slamming the back door. Rather she, with that smile that worried me, held out her hand and said, "Let's have it". I knew instantly someone had called her on the telephone about me winning the drawing. I couldn't believe it, I was about to lose the only prize I had ever won! With a false hope I said, "Have what?" Mom said, "You know what, the drawing card." I removed the slightly wrinkled and concaved card from my rear pocket, which said "Drawing Winner" with my name and twenty five dollars on the front and a thirty three cent debit for three six cent Cokes and three five cent bags of salted peanuts signed by Murph. Mom said, "I see you already spent some of it," after looking at the card. Dad asked, "What did he buy, Martha?" Mom answered, "Three Cokes and three bags of peanuts." Dad said, "Well Martha, at least he should be able to buy something, he won!" Mom eased up and said, "Bryan, I'll keep this until next Saturday and you, Anson, and I will go to the Ross Shop and I'll buy you both some new school clothes." "Oh Mom," I said, and walked into the living room where Dizzy and Pee-wee were telling fans what went wrong at second base. In the summer time my dad liked to watch baseball on the TV. This game must not have been interesting; he didn't bring his coffee in the living room to drink. I took a pillow from the sofa and laid down on the floor in front of the television set wondering what I could have done with the remaining twenty four dollars and sixty seven cents.

Chapter 6
Seventh Grade

I couldn't figure any way around it. I was going to wear the new blue jeans the first day of school. It was my money, or... was my money, and Mom was determined to buy those stupid jeans that had the reinforcement at the knees. It was like running with a stove pipe in your pant leg! Besides, the jeans with the reinforced knees never "broke in" like good jeans. I hated them. The only thing good was Anson had to wear the same kind to school, although style didn't have much bearing on a guy in the first grade.

Huck and I were both in the seventh grade. The seventh grade was all new to us because we were at the high school and moved from class to class throughout the day. Some of the teachers were better than others but the absolute best classes were when the normal teacher was absent and we had a substitute. This held especially true if the substitute teacher was young and a woman. Our first class taught by a substitute teacher was a history class held in a classroom at the east end of the hall on the second floor. The teacher's name was Miss Holt, a young lady just out of college with very little teaching experience other than her student teaching while still in college. This was one of the few times everybody looked forward to class.

We rushed to the classroom with anticipation, looking forward to the challenge of causing a teacher to question their choice of profession. It was noisy. The teacher was seated behind the desk and we all took our seats as the bell rang. She rose and we became semi-quiet as she introduced herself as Miss Holt. She said she would be our teacher for the day because Mrs. Handley was away on personal business. Miss Holt said smiling, "I look forward to getting to know you and an interesting class today." That was good, because we all were looking forward to an "interesting" class too. She, still standing, said, "Let's start by you telling me your names, starting in the back row, the young lady in the white sweater, will you please start by introducing yourself?" Sandy smiles and says, "My name is Sandy Zachary." We all took turns and it became my turn then Barney's. We were seated in alphabetical order and I'm sure I wasn't the only one who thought that we should have picked seats rather than being assigned seats. I'm sure a few of us guys would like to be in the back row, I know I'd would of!

Miss Holt moved behind the desk and took her seat and opened the teacher's copy of *American History*. I heard a fake cough that seemed to come from the second row in the back, it sounded like Huck. I turned just enough to see him from the corner of my eye and he smiled. I knew something was up but didn't know just what. I was seated where I couldn't communicate clandestinely, so about all I could do was acknowledge the unknown. The teacher ask, "Please open your textbooks to page forty-three, and we will begin reading." After the commotion of opening books, dropping assorted items, scooting of chairs, and a few coughs, Miss Holt said, "Sandy, will you please read the first paragraph for us?" Zachary read, then the teacher said, "Mike, please read the next paragraph," and on through the entire class we all took turns reading. I thought it was a noise from outside, although it was strange enough that I turned slightly to look, and got a devilish smile from Huck. It was a hum; classmates seated in the rear of the room were humming! A drone like a thousand yellow jackets! Even the girls were humming! Participation migrated to the front of the classroom and Miss Holt quickly got up and said, "Students that will be enough!" Well there was a slight decrease in overall volume but the humming continued. She picked up a ruler that was lying next to her teachers guide edition of *American History* and briskly slapped her desk. "Who's doing that?" she asked. The humming had stopped but her anger regarding the situation continued to escalate. Her face was red and I could see a vein in her neck bulge in rhythm with her increasing heart beat, as we all exchanged smiles and nods of approval. Miss Holt then asks Sandy, "Sandy, are you doing that?" Naturally, Sandy said no as twenty-three others were soon to do. The substitute teacher worked her way from the back row until she reached me. I was seated directly in front of her desk and it should have been evident that I alone wasn't responsible for the resounding buzz of dozen nests of mad hornets. But, I just couldn't help myself because when Miss Holt ask, "Bryan, did you make that noise?" I responded, with the overall support and laughter of my classmates, "Yes, I was making that noise Miss Holt." She was infuriated and told me to leave the classroom. I closed my book and picked up my other things and looked at the rest of my fellow classmates, smiled, and made my way into the hallway just as the bell rang. The class room emptied behind me with some classmates slapping me on the back as I waited for Huck to exit.

Huck made it into the hallway and we started walking down the stairway to our lockers located behind the bleachers on the lower floor. He said his most used phrase, "Well, what do you think now?" I shrugged my shoulders and said, "I don't know. That teacher may tell the principal, and then I'll be in trouble." "Well if you make it through eighth period study hall it means she didn't tell him," Huck said, as we made our way down the stairs and behind the bleachers in the old gym. We both put our history books in our lockers and I took my science book out for study hall. I'm not sure what Huck took. We made our way back upstairs to the study hall for the last period of the day. Huck and I sat at the same table next to the fire escape door where Bob was already sitting. Bob asked us if we were going to the football game. It was a "soap game." A soap game was a practice game between our own school players and the admission was a bar of soap. The soap was used through the school year in the locker room showers. Huck said, "Yeah, if my parents will let me." I said, "I planned to go." I looked forward to joining the football team but you needed to be a freshman. I had a year to wait.

Huck rode his bike into town after he completed his chores Friday. I invited him to eat with us. It was still daylight and Dad just arrived home. Mom was fixing supper early because she knew dad would want to go to the game. Dad came into the house and sat his lunch pail and Stanley thermos where he always did, in front of the basement door, and took his place at the kitchen table. Mom had his coffee waiting for him and he asks her, "Do you want to go to the football game tonight?" Mom said, "Yes, I'll go." I don't think she really wanted to but it was a way to get away for an evening, and she would enjoy that aspect of the outing. Huck and I planned to walk to the high school. That way, we could go up town after the game. We didn't worry about taking any soap because we would walk to the field located on the north side of the high school, and cut through an adjoining family's yard, therefore by-passing the old fifty-five gallon drum painted blue that was used to collect the bars of soap. The soap bars would come in handy in a few weeks as Halloween approached. It was comfortable knowing a supply of bars were available in the locker room. It was also good to acquire it at the school because none would show up missing from the shelf in the bathroom at home used to store towels, soap, and such items.

Only two quarters were played in the soap game and the game was over. We left just before it ended so we would get to the Highway Café before it got busy. We walked towards the fire house which was just behind the Library. We briskly walked because we wanted to arrive at the Highway Café before the counter was crowded. We walked between the Library and Legion and onto Main Street. When we reached the locker plant we broke into a trot towards Dick Lake's, then ran across the street towards Hawk Eye's and down to the Café. There were two seats available at the counter and we seated ourselves. I knew what I wanted and so did Huck. Crutchy came walking down towards us wearing his customary white apron folded at the waist with the top half neatly tucked under. From behind the counter Crutchy ask, "What will you have boys?" I said, "A chocolate milk shake and an order of fries," and Huck said the same. Crutchy walked down the counter to a small window at the far end and told the cook, "Two fries," and returned to the milk shake mixer and removed two large stainless steel containers from a supply setting under the counter top. He put three scoops of vanilla ice cream, some milk, and chocolate syrup into each container and positioned them on the mixer with a light green top and flipped the switch on. With a whine somewhat like an electric drill and an egg beater the mixer churned away, as Crutchy repositioned both shiny containers causing the whine to change pitch. Just as fast as it started he turned off the mixer and turned towards us with two large heavy glass milk shake glasses which he sat down in front of Huck and me. Turning again, he took the stainless steel containers off the mixer and pivoted as he took one step positioning his body against the counter and poured the contents into the glasses leaving the containers set beside them with a second portion in them. The small counter bell rang just at the right time signaling that our fries were ready to be served. Crutchy went to the end of the counter and returned with us each a large white plate with two thin green lines around the circumference full of golden french fries. I took a long draw through the straw and the coldness of the milk shake made my head hurt. Huck was eating his fries. We both didn't talk much while we consumed our shake and fries with passion. Crutchy was at the cash register so we both paid him, a quarter for the milk shake and twenty cents for the fries, expensive but well worth it.

The juke box had just stopped and people were still coming in the restaurant, mostly school kids. Huck had a nickel left over and knew I did too. He suggested that we both put them in the juke box. One record was five cents but if you deposited a dime you could select three records. I put my nickel in the machine and Huck followed. He selected *"Love Potion No. 9."* I moved front and center looking at the title cards brightly illuminated from underneath although I knew what song I was going to select, *Louie Louie*. *Love Potion No. 9* had already started to play before we decided on the third song, *The Stroll*. We both stood in front of the juke box as others filed in through the door. Huck decided it was time to turn up the volume of the juke box. Crutchy didn't like for the music to be too loud so it was best to turn it up in increments. Huck reached behind the machine to the secret volume control just as *Love Potion No. 9* stopped and the machine was searching for the next 45 RPM record. With no music playing it was difficult to set the volume at a safe level. Just as Huck removed his arm from behind the machine the unmistakable lead in to *Louie Louie* started. I looked at Huck and he at me. We both knew in a second it was going to be loud! We started to move away from the juke box but it was too late. The song had started and the windows were shaking! Crutchy spotted us and gave us a look that we were accustom to but not comfortable in receiving. We slowly made our way to the steamed-up plate glass window and door where the football players were filing in as Crutchy leaned and reached behind the juke box and lowered the volume. He was close to us so we thought it was best to leave. We were sad that we couldn't stay long enough to hear our songs but under the circumstances….safety was always the best policy!

Huck and I stood in front of the Highway for a while before we decided to walk the short distance to the Playhouse. The street was strangely quiet now and so was the Playhouse. There were a few older girls sitting in booths but a totally different atmosphere than the Highway. We looked through the window and didn't go in. We were broke anyway. We decided to head for my house where Huck had left his bicycle. As we walked north on Washington Street I mimicked the song, *Blue Moon*,

"Da-ta-ta- dah, dang-a-dang dang, Ding-dong-ding, Blue Moon….."

In less than ten minutes, we were approaching the witch house. Usually we tried to avoid it, when it was dark, unless we had formed a small army; it was just Huck and I. As we got closer our mood changed from happy-go-lucky to somber and quiet. Huck said in almost a whisper, "What do you think now?" I said, "Let's cross over to the other side of the street," which we did, but not before Huck had pitched a rock which noisily skipped across the witch's porch. We both broke into a fast run towards my house not slowing down until we were crossing our yard towards the back door. Huck and I sat on the steps of the back door, allowing him to gain the composure for his long bicycle ride home. Reluctantly, Huck walked over to his bike and said, "I'll see you at school Monday."

Chapter 7
The Horse Ride

The grass was turning from a light brown to small patches of green on the south side of the garage, several crocuses were standing up pledging their allegiance to the warm rays of the spring sun, and Rose Ann smiled at me! I was heading towards Mrs. Kile's math class and unexpectedly, Rose Ann looked at me, not a passing glance, but she looked me directly in the eyes and smiled. Usually I would have turned away at the first sign of expression, but I was almost ready to move on to the ninth grade and something about that smile intrigued me. Rose Ann had dark hair fixed in two pony tails, one on each side of her head. She had freckles on her nose and cheeks. Huck was a distant cousin, although I never knew exactly how.

A few days passed, it was Saturday, and I was hoping Dad would go fishing, and maybe I could go too. He had said something to Mom about how good a mess of crappie would taste so my expectations were running high. It was a beautiful spring day. Just as I had hoped, he came out in the back yard where I had my bicycle upside down, turning the pedals, and watching the back wheel go around and around. Dad said, "Hoss, you want to go

53

fishing with me?" I said, "Yah, now?" He said, "Yes, run in and tell your mother that you are going with me, then get your stuff gathered up." I ran in the house and yelled, "Mom, Mom!" She answered, "Yes…." I cut her off saying, "Dad wants me to go fishing with him, I'll see you later." The screen door barely had the time to slam shut when I pushed it open and ran to the garage to get my pole and tackle box. I ran to Dads pickup parked in the drive where he was loading his tackle in the bed. He took my pole and tackle box from me and put it in the bed too. He asked, "Did you tell your mother?" I said, "Yes" and away we went. The lake was just north of town. Huck lived east of it and I couldn't help to think about Rose Ann who lived just north. The smile in the school hallway a few days before still had me curious.

Dad slowly drove down the lane that leads to the lake, arrived at the turnaround point, and parked the truck. We took our tackle and walked to our john boat which was turned upside down on the bank. Dad laid his pole, tackle box, and sculling paddle down and carefully and slowly turned the boat over being vigilant for any snakes that may have claimed it as a home. Everything looked good so he slipped the boat into the water about halfway and stepped into the bow. I handed him his stuff and crouching, he went to the seat in the rear and sat down. The bow was lightened by his weight in the rear and I could move the boat easily. I laid my pole and tackle box on the floor of the aluminum boat and put one knee on the front seat and pushed off with the other leg. The boat quietly entered the water all but the small splash that the toe of my tennis shoe made as I swung it around and over the side. Dad didn't say anything about the extra commotion. He had taught me to think like a fish and fish didn't like any unusual commotion. He maneuvered the boat parallel with the bank and readied his pole. I saw he had a pinkie on. A pinkie was a small jig with a bright pink head with white hair tail used primarily for crappie. I opened my tackle box and tied one on using the special knot he had taught me. He had a very small red and white bobber positioned about two and a half feet above the pinkie he had tied on. I found one that had turned dull rolling around in the bottom of my tackle box and pushed the button exposing the small brass hook that I carefully passed the line under allowing almost the same distance between the pinkie and the bobber that dad had on his. He slowly moved the boat with the sculling paddle. Dad was headed out to the first brush pile. Crappie liked brush piles. Prematurely, I made a cast towards the brush pile only to throw too far causing the jig to drop in the middle of the brush and the little bobber to strike a branch and spin around it many times. Dad seeing what I did said, "Balls! You can just sit there and wait until I fish around the brush." I felt really bad. I wanted so much to be like Dad and I made a stupid mistake already, and we hadn't even got a good start. Suddenly, Dad hooked into a fish! He laid the paddle on the seat by his leg and started carefully reeling in the fish. He maneuvered the fish to the side of the boat, which was only about three inches above the water and used his thumb and index finger to lift the fish over the side of the boat. Dad with a smile on his face said, "This is what we are looking for." He quickly caught two more and after he had placed the last fish in the fish basket tied onto the unused oar lock just about halfway between him and I, he said, "Let's go and get your line untangled."

Skillfully keeping the boat parallel with the bank we were slowly in route to the next brush pile, a tree that had fallen in the water. I knew it would be a "honey hole" so I rehearsed my upcoming cast towards it in my mind. We were within easy casting range; I drew back my rod and looked behind myself to make sure I wasn't going to hook anything in or out of the boat with my back cast when I saw her! It was Rose Ann on her horse! She was across the narrow finger of water on a rise above the bank silhouetted by a few puffy white clouds and blue sky. Dad noticed I didn't complete my cast and ask, "Who is that?" I was embarrassed so I lied and said, "I don't know." She sat there for just a few minutes and when I looked again she disappeared over the hill. Dad and I caught a mess of crappie that Saturday morning but I couldn't get Rose Ann off my mind. We had fried fish and hush puppies that evening.

Huck came up to me behind the bleachers before class Monday morning and said, "Look at what I have!" He pulled a great looking green snake from his shirt pocket. I asked, "Can I hold him?" Huck handed the snake to me. It was thinner than a pencil and about as long. It entwined my fingers and I looked down the aisle for an un-expecting girl to scare. I thought of Rose Ann. I didn't want to scare her, but other than that, I was unsure what I wanted. The only thing I knew for certain was I couldn't forget her smile last week or her sitting on that horse Saturday. I gave Huck his green snake back and he threaded it into his shirt pocket. The first bell rang and we hurriedly climbed the stairs to the second floor and Mrs. Harden's English class.

I was looking at the class pictures hanging high above the lockers on the second floor as I made my way to English class. I always enjoyed looking at the class pictures. Pictures were displayed from the time the building was built to last years graduating class. I was studying the faces of Class 1952 when I bumped into someone in the hall. It was Rose Ann! With a slight measure of delight, I tried to twist and step past her without looking totally frightened. She quickly countered my move by repositioning herself countering my evasive actions. I wasn't going to get around her before she accomplished whatever she was planning. I stopped, and before I could think of something to say, Rose Ann, with a smile said, "I want you to take this." She removed something she had tucked between her plaid skirt and shiny back belt and as she handed it to me I realized it was a note folded into a small triangle. Then she said, "Let me know." I had no idea what she wanted but she stepped aside as I put the small folded up paper in my front jean pocket and entered the classroom.

I made my way to my assigned seat and opened my English text book. The last bell rang and Mrs. Harden said, "Good morning class." We responded with a good morning, hello, morning, and several indistinguishable responses. I had waited long enough! The anticipation was unbearable. I removed the neatly folded note from my pocket and held it in my palm not to arouse suspicion from Christine who would take special delight in discovering what I had in my hand. Christine sat on my right and Katie on the other side. I wasn't happy over the seating arrangements but had no choice in the selection. Mrs. Harden had been a teacher for many years and she assigned our seating in the classroom with the upmost skill. She placed us beside people that we normally wouldn't choose to sit by in a million years. She knew what she was doing and we knew it. I needed to be very careful with the note. I held it long enough that it was getting moist from my perspiration. I needed to make a move soon. I ever so carefully looked at Christine and she appeared occupied in adding embellishments to a heart that occupied half of her notebooks inside leaf. She had a mad crush on a guy that was a junior. So while she was drawing little hearts around the edge of the large heart and dreaming about her guy I turned and took a quick peak at Katie. She was listening to Mrs. Harden and ready to take notes. I opened my notebook and placed the English text book on the right side of it. I held up the left side at an angle to block Christine's inquisitive eyes and carefully opened the note. It read, "Bryan, Would you like to come to my house Saturday morning? We can ride my horse. Let me know by this time tomorrow. Love, Rose Ann." She signed it, "Love!" I carefully refolded the note and placed it back in my jean pocket.

I was very excited about the way Rose Ann signed the note. I wanted to get it out again and look at it! I had been lucky because Christine hadn't detected it but her instinct must have interrupted her day dream about the junior. She had repositioned herself in her chair allowing herself to have a better view of my notebook. My concealed excitement wasn't concealed from Christine. She was watching me like a hawk so my opportunity to take another look at Rose Ann's note had vanished at least until the end of English class.

The bell rang and we filed out of the classroom as orderly as eight graders normally would, with a few elbows and shoves. Morning study hall was next and I already had my science book so I made it to the study hall as fast as I could and picked an unusual desk. I hoped this desk, close to the study hall teacher's desk, would allow me to look at the note again. Bob noticed me sitting there and as he approached said, "Hay Hoss, You in trouble?" I answered, "No, why?" I knew why he may have thought I was in trouble. It was stupid of me to select that table so I shrugged my shoulders, picked up my books and followed

Bob to the table on the other side of the room just past the study hall main doors. Bob and I joined Tank who was already seated.

The third bell rang and the noise and confusion subsided to a tolerable state. Tank waited for the noise level to decrease just a little more then made a fake cough. By the sound of the cough almost everyone knew it was fake. A few guys snickered and the girls simply ignored it with the exception of Elaine rolling her eyes, a sign directed toward Tank, implying his stupidity. He replied to her with another cough. I was anxious to look at the note again. I acted amused at Tank when in reality I was only interested in reading that grand document for the second time. Tank enticed Bob to make a fake cough as well as Terry, who was sitting at the table by the fire escape door. A few other random coughs were heard and then Tank made a mistake. He made a noise but it didn't sound like a cough. It sounded like someone was frightened out of their socks and screamed! Everyone became quiet as Mrs. Heath, the study hall teacher for the week said, "Jerry, (Tank's real name) do you feel better now?" Everyone including many girls laughed, especially when Mrs. Heath's question rendered him speechless.

After a few minutes which seemed like an eternity, I removed the note from my pocket and secretly unfolded it below the table. I read it again and quickly refolded it and returned it to my pocket. How was I going to answer her, with a note or ask someone to relay a message? I didn't have the courage to approach her in person. I decided to go with a note and ask Zachary to give it to Rose Ann. Zachary sat in front of me in science class and she and I got along well. Most importantly she could be trusted to not tell anyone. The bell rang and I remained in my seat acting like I had been caught off guard, I tore off the corner, about a quarter of the page, of note book paper and wrote a note. I wrote, "Rose Ann, What time do you want me to come? Let me know. I'll be there. Bryan," and carefully folded the note into a square that could be easily concealed. I left the class room and headed down the hall to the science room. Science was my favorite class. Our Teacher, Mr. Topping, required students to draw the subjects of his lectures and label them. Drawing was easy for me and I also had good penmanship for an eighth grade boy, therefore, I made my best grades in his class. Drawing one-celled amebas and labeling their anatomy was an assignment I enjoyed. I immediately went to my seat and whispered to Zachary, "Will you deliver a note for me?" She said, "Yes, who to?" I said, "This is top secret! You've got to promise that you won't tell anyone." She said, "I promise. Who do you want me to deliver it to?" I was almost afraid to say but finally mumbled, "Rose Ann." Zachary held out her hand and I gave her the tightly folded note, and reminded her, "It's top secret!" She gave me a reassuring smile. I trusted Zachary.

Today we had tests in English and History class. What a way to end a week! I knew I had not studied history and just managed to struggle through my inadequate notes I took through the week in English class hoping for the best. Huck and I were heading downstairs to our lockers when I saw Zachary. She raised her index finger and tapped her right temple, a sign she knew something. I told Huck I forgot something and turned around looking back at Zachery. When Huck started up the stairway I quickly went to Zachary. She said, "Rose Ann said she will look for you around one o'clock." I thanked her and ran to catch up with Huck.

On Saturday, I rode my bicycle down Mule Hill to the highway. I stopped waiting on a chance to cross when fear flooded over me and I considered turning around, going home, and forgetting about Rose Ann. The traffic presented an opportunity to cross and I rose off the seat and pumped hard to cross the highway as fast as I could. It felt good to be across the highway but that good feeling was replaced with apprehension. I didn't have any horse experience and less woman experience! The mile to Rose Ann's went quickly. I pulled off the gravel road almost losing my balance as I crossed the ridge of rocks pushed to the side by car and farm truck traffic and stopped in her driveway at the end of the sidewalk. Rose Ann came out and with a smile said, "Follow me." I laid my bike down on the grass beside the sidewalk and followed her toward the barn. I didn't notice the size of the large barn as much as the large imposing horse standing in the board fenced lot in front and to the left of the large red faded structure. I lingered behind Rose Ann, as she approached the horse. She put both hands on the top board of the fence, turned to see me standing a safe distance back and said, "What's the matter, you scared?" I told her, "No, I'm not scared. I just wanted to see what you were going to do." She climbed up the fence and sat on the top facing the barn, whistled and her horse came slowly towards her. She reached out and the horse was close enough that she stroked him above the nose and reaching into her jean pocket, with her other hand, pulled out a sugar cube and gave it to the horse which she called Jim. I was standing on the top of the bottom board with my hands on the second to the top board. Rose Ann knew I was frightened. She took pity on me and said, "Come up here, Jim is gentle." I smiled and said, "OK," but didn't move.

Rose Ann jumped off the board fence and ran to the barn and returned with a bridle. She climbed over the fence and walked up to Jim and put the bit in his mouth and adjusted the bridle. She positioned Jim next to the fence and climbed back up to the third board and gracefully mounted Jim. She rode the large reddish brown horse bareback around the coral then stopped next to the fence between where I was and a large water tank on the other side of the fence. She said, "Climb over the fence and hold on to the top board and stand on the edge of the water tank. I'll ride Jim close and then get on behind me." I ask, "What do I hang on to?" Rose Ann laughed and said, "Me, silly!" That pushed me over the edge. I positioned myself just like she had instructed. Rose Ann brought Jim next to the water tank and I threw my right leg over him and positioned myself using Rose Ann's waist to steady myself. She made two clicks with her mouth and cheek and Jim stepped out. I intensified my hold on Rose Ann's waist and tried to stabilize myself using my legs against the horse's sides. It happened so fast! I was up, off, and in the water tank! The water was cold and I came to my senses quickly to see Rose Ann sitting on Jim, laughing at me. I didn't know what to say. She said with laughter, "Are you OK?" I replied, "I think so." I climbed out of the tank soaked from head to foot and made it over the board fence. I turned around just in time to see Rose Ann give Jim another sugar cube.

I was feeling about as low as a guy can feel. Rose Ann tied the horse to the top fence board and climbed over. She stood there with her hands on her hips looking at me and giggled. She quickly said, "I'm sorry," and we walked towards the house. My shoes were making a sloshing noise with each step. We reached the sidewalk and my bicycle, where I sat down on the grass and pulled my shoes off and dumped the water out. I was suffering from acute embarrassment as I sat there not saying a word. Rose Ann stooped down to my level, smiled and said, "That wasn't bad." It couldn't have been worse but, I trusted her judgment. I put my shoes back on and stood up raising my bicycle at the same time. Then out of the blue Rose Ann asks, "Do you want to go steady?" It took all the fortitude I could muster to answer her, weakly I replied, "Ok." I swung my leg over my bike and down the drive I went. Just as I got to the road I prepared for the ridge of gravel and turned toward Rose Ann and waved goodbye. She waved back and ran into the house. I didn't notice the wet clothes during the ride home.

After the Ed Sullivan Show on Sunday evening I thought about returning to school and my buddies finding out about me "Going Steady" with Rose Ann. Everything went fine at school until Huck and I were going down the hall to English class. Just before we got to the classroom door Rose Ann stepped out in front of us. I did the only thing I could do. I maneuvered around her and tried not to make eye contact. I knew I would be confronted before the day was over. Sure enough, during lunch hour Bob, Huck, and I were sitting half way up the bleachers in the old gym when Rose Ann walked by. I knew she wanted to catch me alone. It wasn't that I didn't like her; I just was unsure and inexperienced regarding such things.

That afternoon Tank and I were standing at the water fountain down the hall from the Science Classroom and Rose Ann saw me again. She left her locker door open and quickly approached me. When she got close it looked like she had been crying. She stopped a short distance away from us and stared at me. She then reached under her belt and removed a note which she hurled at me only it hit Tank on the shoulder. She ran back to her locker and closed the door and disappeared down the hall. I picked up the note and put it in my pocket. I had a good idea what it said. Tank said, "What was that all about?" I said, "I'll tell you later," hoping he would forget about the incident as we walked towards the Science Classroom.

Soon after the class started I carefully opened the note which read, "I'm sorry. I hope we can still be friends. Rose Ann."

Chapter 8
The Whistle

A pep rally was scheduled half way through seventh hour study hall. We would be dismissed early and were to assemble in the new gymnasium. The pep band and cheerleaders would be dismissed ten minutes before three and the rest of us would be dismissed at three o'clock. We made our way to the new gym and heard our school song being played by the twelve piece ensemble. Tank, Bob, Huck, and I sat close to the pep band because they were on the north end of the bleachers and close to the band and locker room door. When the pep rally was over we could be some of the first to leave. All the students filed in taking seats in the bleachers and the basketball team sat on folding chairs next to a portable podium positioned on the center court stripe.

The principal, Mr. Tucker made his way to the podium and held his hand up to silence the pep band and the students. The pep band quit playing *"On Wisconsin"*, our adopted school song, but the students continued to cheer and yell not necessarily in support of the basketball team but to irritate Mr. Tucker. Finally, we quieted down and the principal started his monotone speech about school spirit and the tradition of our sports program. All we could think about was, it was less than twenty minutes to dismissal. It became exceptionally quiet that afternoon with the whole student body assembled together at one time. Huck decided to take advantage of the moment. He elbowed me and removed a small shiny metal tube about six inches long from his sock and proudly showed it to me and smiled the kind of smile that indicated something was going to happen. Huck then removed a small gray and black tube that was marked Dasey. I knew what this was, BB's. He looked around to make sure no one was watching and tipped the round cardboard container and emptied some BB's into his mouth. Mr. Tucker was talking about sportsmanship and our behavior at tonight's game, boring us to death, and Huck took aim on the center of the bass drum. I heard a puff of air and a split second later a boom. Huck had hit his intended target and we all were surprised at the results, especially Greg, the bass drum player! Everyone broke into laughter except Greg and Mr. Tucker. The principal again held his hands up and eventually the laughter subsided when Huck raised the metal tube up to his mouth and fired another shot hitting the bass drum dead center again! Greg's face turned red, the student body howled with laughter, and Mr. Tucker just stood there with his hands placed on his hips, staring above us at the wall behind the bleachers. When things settled down again Mr. Tucker said, "Greg, please take your instrument to the band room!" The laughter resumed as Greg left the gym.

Mr. Tucker said Coach Bennett was called away and introduced the Assistant Coach, Mr. Burns. Nearly everyone liked Coach Burns. His demeanor resembled an equal mix between Dean Martin and Red Skelton. The Assistant Coach approached the podium and exclaimed,

"Let's go Blue!" to the cheers of the student body. Then the bell rang, and without any more fanfare we all quickly made our way out. We went through the locker room and stopped outside just long enough to congratulate Huck on his target selection!

I left my buddies and hurriedly made my way through the student parking lot, cut through Gordon's back yard and headed home, a ten minute walk down the "Alley." The Alley was a street with only two houses that ran about three and one half blocks. Much of the west side of the street was farm ground and the east side was the back yards of residents on Washington Street. I saw someone walking ahead at a distance far enough away I couldn't tell who it was but I figured it was Gaiter. I ran to get closer and I could tell it was him so I let loose with a crow call and he stopped and turned around. Gaiter waited for me as I ran to join him. I ask Gaiter what he thought about the drumming and he said, "What drumming? What are you talking about?" "Didn't you hear it?" I asked. Gaiter looked surprised and said, "No, Tom and I hid in the band room and left a little early. What happened?" I told him about Huck shooting the bass drum with his BB pea shooter. Gaiter laughed and asked, "Are you going to the game tonight?" I said, "Yes, I'm meeting Tank at Murph's and we are going from there. Do you want to go with us?" "Nah," Gaiter said, "I've got to meet Tom in front of the Baptist Church, but I'll see you there." We reached my driveway and I said to Gaiter, "I'll see you later."

I opened the back door and Mom was at the kitchen counter carefully scooping coffee into the percolator. Dad would be home soon. It felt good to be home because there was a nip in the air outside. I wanted to tell Mom about the drum but decided it would be best if I didn't. Mom asks, "Bryan, you are going to the game tonight, aren't you?" I replied, "Yes, we talked about that Wednesday." She smiled and said, "I guess I forgot."

Anson was in the living room, lying in front of the television watching *Huckaberry Hound.* I stepped over him and turned the channel knob on the set to channel ten. I didn't know what was on ten but I found it necessary to let Anson know who was going to control the TV, at least until after supper. Then Dad would watch Walter Cronkite. Anson let out a mournful "Mom!" And mom yelled from the kitchen, "Bryan, leave Anson alone!"

Dad arrived home and had his coffee and cigarette as mom set the table. Soon we all sat down and ate. Dad asked me if I was still going to the game, and I told him yes. He told me to be home by nine thirty. I gave him a look of disgust and he instantly replied, "If you continue to look at me like that you can spend the night in your room!" Anson set across from me with his stupid grin. I said, with a slight smile, "I'm sorry, I'll be home by then. Can I be excused?" Mom said, "You may," and I got out of the kitchen. I didn't want to risk saying or doing something else that might anger dad. With Anson slyly making faces at me I knew there was a possibility of things boiling over and I would find myself spending the evening upstairs or possibly worse.

I met Tank at Murphs. We both walked because we didn't want to leave our bicycles unattended at the high school. Some upperclassmen might think it was funny to let the air out of our tires or worse. Tank was still laughing about Huck shooting the bass drum. He was telling Bob about it. Bob had a detention for baaing like a lamb in math class and wasn't allowed to attend the pep rally. I asked Bob if he planned on going to the game. He said he was so we started down the alley behind the north side of Main Street towards the high school. As we neared the school people were already arriving. We were playing our arch rivals, the Warriors from a town just six miles west. We walked to the parking lot and behind the gymnasium to the visiting team's locker room door. Our plan was to walk quickly through the visiting team's locker room to the door directly across the room that opened into the gym avoiding the twenty five cent student admission. We looked at one another and Tank turned with Bob and me close behind. It just took a second and we were standing at the north end of the gym on the visitor's side. We walked across the shiny floor next to the out of bounds line, under the goal to The Bluestreaks side. The teams were getting their last minute instructions so we increased our pace. I saw Gaiter and Tom standing by the band door next to the end of the bleachers. I waved at them and climbed, following Bob and Tank to the top row. It was a good place to sit because you could lean back against the wall and it also was a good view. I looked down towards the band room and didn't see Gaiter or Tom. I was wondering where they went and just then I saw a hand appear on the bleacher's varnished seat about five rows up. Then it slipped off and another hand which was unmistakably the match to the first hand appeared and disappeared just as quickly. Another hand appeared that had a temporary ink pen tattoo, it was Gaiter's! I recognized the tattoo because I saw it that afternoon when we were walking home. I knew they had some sort of plan, a reason for going under the bleachers but wasn't sure what it may have been. The bleachers were the kind that pulled out from the wall. They were pushed back against the wall when the extra space was required within the gymnasium. Because of their design, you could get under them quite easily. Another thing, the seats and floor boards had gaps large enough that you could see out from inside the dark confines beneath, but people couldn't see in.

It was a very close game, never more than four points separated us and our arch rivals. There was less than two minutes until the half and both the visiting and home crowds were very excited, standing and cheering the teams. We received the ball due to a turnover and were making a fast break down the court when a whistle stopped play at half court. Monty disgustedly bounced the ball to the referee standing close to him with a look of disbelief and question on his face. The ref trotted to the middle of the floor and met with the two other officials. The spectators raised the noise level a notch and quickly the ref that had the ball stepped out of bounds at mid-court and indicated we had the ball. The visitors booed and we cheered. The Blue's coach was hot. He was trying to get an explanation from the ref but the referee didn't offer one. We missed our shot and they got the rebound. The teams quickly reversed direction and just as the ball was passed across mid court the whistle was blown again. The team member who caught the ball dropped it and held both hands out toward the ref closest to him, the same one as before. He was a human question mark if there ever was one. The ref quickly walked to the ball and again met with his staff. They all three approached the timekeepers desk located at mid court. Just then it dawned upon me! Gaiter and Tommy….. They must have a whistle! I elbowed Tank and he turned saying, "What?" I said laughing, "I think Gaiter and Tommy took a whistle under the bleachers!" Bob leaned over to join our conversation and ask, "What's going on?" I again said, "I think Gaiter and Tommy have a whistle under the bleachers!" The refs signaled to the teams to resume play. The crowd was going bananas! The refs didn't explain anything which infuriated both benches. The Warriors made a two pointer and we threw the ball in bounds. As Barney reached mid-court, the play stopped again due to the phantom whistle. The referees immediately went to the time keeper and official scorer. Our principal, Mr. Tucker was sitting just beside the time keeper and official score keepers table and joined the assembled group of officials, as well as the Blue's Coach Bennett. The Warrior Coach started to cross the floor when Mr. Tucker left the sideline and positioned himself in the jump circle at mid-court. One ref was tying to explain something to our coach, Mr. Bennett, and one other went to the Warriors coach which hadn't made it across the floor yet. They walked back towards their bench. Mr. Tucker stood in the center of the gym floor, finally raising his hand as to ask for quiet. The fans after considerable coaching from the referees, coaching staff, and cheerleaders became quiet enough that Mr. Tucker made this announcement: "Apparently someone has chosen to disrupt the game. On behalf of our guests and our loyal fans, we apologize. We will resume the game but before we do, we ask that whoever is guilty of disrupting the game quit blowing the whistle. If caught, you will be escorted by the police, off the school property and properly dealt with." The crowd cheered and the referee blew the whistle and signaled for play to resume. As Mr. Tucker was walking off the court I turned to see Gaiter and Tommy exit the band room door. It was them!

We left with four minutes left in the fourth quarter. The Blue were twelve points behind. A light cool rain had started which inspired us to increase our pace towards the Highway Café. We were some of the first students there. In fifteen or twenty minutes the Highway, as well as the Playhouse, would be jumping. Tank ordered fries and a cherry Coke, Bob a chocolate milk shake. I ordered a chocolate shake too. Crutchy prepared the ice cream, milk, and chocolate in the large stainless steel containers and put them both on the light green topped mixer. He gave each a twist to make sure they were sealed and turned on the motor. Then he sat the heavy glasses in front of Bob and me, turned around and shut off the mixer motor. Crutchy retrieved a glass from under the counter and pumped cherry syrup into the bottom of the glass then filled the class with Coke from the fountain. He placed the cherry Coke in front of Tank and Tank said, "Thanks Crutchy." Crutchy said, "Your welcome. Who won the game?" Tank said, "We were loosing by twelve points when we decided to leave." Crutchy turned and sat the shakes in front of Bob and me and poured the glasses full, stuck a straw in both and said, "Enjoy."

It was getting colder because the large plate glass window facing Main Street was getting foggy. We couldn't see what was happening outside but I did notice Rose Ann enter the restaurant with three other girls. She looked at me, as I sat at the counter, and to relieve the wave of despair that swept over me in that instant, I curled my nose and raised it towards the tin ceiling. I secretly wished we could re-establish "going steady."

Tank slurped the last drop of cherry Coke making a loud sucking sound with his straw. Bob and I both had about an inch or so of shake left and we both took turns seeing who could make the loudest slurp. We waited to see what the next song was going to play on the juke box. It was "*Locomotion*," some girl must have played it. We all three looked at one another and without saying a word left the Highway.

The light rain had subsided to a foggy mist. Tank said, "Let's check out what's going on at Murph's." Checking the time on the bank clock I answered, "Ok!" We walked down the south side of Main Street and stopped in front of the Playhouse. The window was steamed up so much we couldn't see who was in there but we could hear *"I'm Sorry"* playing on the juke box. We walked past Burger's and looked across the street at The Corner, a hardware store like Burger's. We crossed Main Street and walked north and for some unknown reason Tank made his way across the street stopping under the awning in front of Wolfe's. Bob and I understood why Tank chose to cross the street when we saw the car. There sat Phillipi's '51 Chevy with the "Cam Busters" car club sign in the back window resting on a bed of white, tufted material that looked like snow but there was no mistake about the intimidation the sign carried. Tank suggested we hang around to see if Phillipi would leave soon. The Chevy had a "split manifold" with glass packs that sounded good, especially when he would rack off. We waited for about five more minutes. Because of the cool mist we decided to head our separate directions. Before parting Bob asked, "Are you guys going to the Drawing tomorrow afternoon?" I answered, "Yes, you guys want to meet at Murphs?" Tank gave thumbs up and seeing him, so did Bob.

It was a cold lonely walk home. I thought about passing the witch house but most of all I thought about Rose Ann. I wish I hadn't of stuck my nose up at her.

Chapter 9
Awakening

It didn't take long to go through the line at the school cafeteria. The rest of the forty-five minutes was spent in the old gym, especially today, an unusually cold and gray November day. The guys, excluding a few juniors and seniors who were sitting with girl friends on the bleachers, were standing along the walls at either end of the gym watching the girls dance to music. Some girls would bring the latest 45's and the school had a RCA record player that was kept on the stage. I think it was meant to be kept in the school library but the librarian appointed someone who was a member of the AV Club to oversee the record player. Dances like the Stroll, and Bunny Hop were popular although a new dance called the Mash Potato was being performed by a few next to the stage.

Huck, Tank, Bob, Terry and I were standing on the east end of the gym because for some unknown reason this end was the cool end. Maybe because it was close to the boys restroom and there was always a chance of a fight or something happening in there. When it was raining and the older guys didn't want to hide in the student parking lot to smoke they would sit on the window sills in the restroom and smoke before the bell. The windows had the kind of glass that was etched, allowing light through but couldn't be seen through. When the smoke would get heavy they would open the windows. The windows were located below the principals' office and opening them was an invitation for him to investigate when the wind was in the right direction.

The first bell rang and someone lifted the tone arm off the record playing and turned off the hi-fi. We all headed to our lockers to get our books. We four had our lockers behind the bleachers. It was darker in the aisle behind the bleachers because they blocked the light and there were few ceiling lights back there. We always entered the passageway with caution. It was a good place for an upper classman to approach and accuse one of us of something, often something we didn't even know about, and swiftly impose a physical punishment. It looked clear today. We opened our combination locks and removed a book or two, slammed the metal doors and hooked the padlock in the handle and with an upward motion, using our open palms, bumped closed the lock. We made our way to the study hall. Many students were assigned study hall after lunch. This arrangement may have allowed the teachers more time for theirs. The second bell found us looking for a good seat, at a table with someone we wanted to sit with. Tank and I went to the same table we usually would sit at, the table next to the door on the far side. I wasn't sure where Huck and Bob were until I saw Bob taking the table next to the fire escape door at the rear of the room with two other guys. Huck joined Mike and two others next to the library door.

The atmosphere was unusually quiet. It was a cool gray November day and the basketball game was away.

We guys thought riding the fan bus wasn't cool so we were not going to the game. Away games didn't leave as much opportunity for fun as home games.

Tank had a nail file he found in the hallway. He placed it on the table edge and flipped it. The thin metal file vibrated and made a louder noise than a ruler usually did and was much easier to conceal from prying eyes of the study hall teacher. He waited until he thought the coast was clear again and made another flip. This time, after the flip, he scooted the file on the slick desk surface making the noisy vibration that started at a low tone rise in pitch.

Mrs. Heath slowly looked over her glasses at our table, nodded her head, and pushed her chair back. Before she rose Mr. Tucker hurriedly entered the study hall and approached her desk. He was a rather small man in stature. Many of us were as big as him, but he carried himself in a way that commanded authority, although today was different. He seemed unsure of himself. His appearance in the study hall was enough to draw our attention but this seemed different. He whispered something to Mrs. Heath and for a teacher that always held her composure, she was visibly upset. You could hear a pin drop. Then Mr. Tucker offered his hand to Mrs. Heath, helping her down the two steps of the raised platform the desk sat on and took the platform himself. Eminently he faced forward and made eye contact with the students assembled and said, "I have a very, very important announcement. I have just received a telephone call advising me that our president, John F. Kennedy has been shot in Dallas, Texas." Students looked at each other in disbelief. He went on to say, "Please stay seated and I'm gong to bring the TV from the library in so we can receive any information available."

He quickly left through the side door into the library

and returned with a small black and white television. He ascended the two steps and placed the set on the teacher's desk facing us while Mrs. Heath struggled with the cord routing it to a socket behind the chair and plugged it in. In the silence, the small set came to life. Walter Cronkite, with an unfamiliar look of concern, was sitting at a desk looking at a paper he was just handed. The veteran newscaster looked up from the paper he was holding and announced, "Here is a bulletin from CBS News. In Dallas, Texas, three shots were fired at President Kennedy's motor cade in downtown Dallas." No one in the room removed their eyes from the television. The report continued with the events of the day leading up to the situation in Dealey Plaza.

Mr. Tucker left the study hall and in a few minutes returned announcing that school would be dismissed for those of us living in town. Students riding busses would be dismissed at their regular time. Those who wanted to stay until 3:15pm could remain in the study hall. Quietly we left the room. There was very little conversation in the halls as we stored our books and took coats from the lockers. We left that November 22nd day to a world that forever would be changed.

It was only about a ten minute walk, if I walked fast, home. I wanted to get there as fast as I could and watch the television. Mom was in the kitchen and met me as I entered the familiar room. She gave me a hug and asked me, "Bryan, are you going to be all right?" I said, "I'm OK, Do you have the television on?" Mom didn't watch much TV and she answered, "No, Jean just called and told me about the President and that school was dismissed early." I went into the living room with my heavy jacket on and turned on the set. I hurriedly removed my coat and threw it on a nearby chair. I heard the televisions familiar crackle and soon the sound and then picture came on showing the dark blue 1961 Presidential Lincoln speeding towards an overpass with Walter explaining the route taken to the hospital. After a pause, Walter Cronkite reading a paper he was just handed, removed his dark framed glasses and slowly put them back on, visibly moved, reported. "From Dallas, Texas, the flash, apparently official. President Kennedy died at 1:00pm CST....."

I felt things were unwinding. I was frightened. I wished Dad was home. I continued to watch television until he arrived home. The first time I had left the living room was to meet Dad in the kitchen. He was home early and mom had not started coffee. Dad and I went into the living room. Anson was playing with Freckles. Freckles was lying under the coffee table and quickly swishing his tail from side to side. Anson was using a tinker-toy stick with a bird feather attached to the end to entice Freckles to pounce on with his claws. Dad sat down in his chair and I laid down on the floor in front of the television. Soon Mom brought Dad a hot cup of coffee. Other than being in the kitchen for supper we stayed glued to the television set until bedtime.

In the morning, there were only special reports, no Saturday morning cartoons, Sky King, or Roy Rodgers. I wasn't disappointed. The recent events had a profound effect upon me, my father and mother and hundreds of thousands of people throughout the world. We were witnessing history in a fashion that hadn't been done before, live television. I was riveted to the set, although I didn't fully understand why, just a burning need to watch!

Sunday morning I woke to hear the TV set. Dad had gotten up early. I dressed and went down stairs. Entering the kitchen Mom asked me if I was going to church and

I told her no. I wanted to see what was going on in Washington. She sat a bowl of oatmeal on the table and I sat down to breakfast. I sprinkled a large amount of sugar on top of the oatmeal and topped it off with some milk. I quickly ate and went into the living room. I ask dad, "Anything going on?" Dad said, "Nothing much new." I took my place in front of the TV. A reporter was talking about the suspect, Lee Harvey Oswald, an employee of the Texas School Book Depository and a rifle the police had recovered.

Dad and I watched until Mom came into the living room to announce that lunch was ready. I wasn't very hungry because I had developed a headache from so much TV that morning. I didn't eat much but Anson made up for it. My younger sister was sitting in her high chair, beside my mother, slapping her hand in mashed potatoes.

I asked to be excused and Mom said, "Bryan, I think you have watched TV enough. Why don't you find something else to do?" I said, "Mom," and returned to the television. A reporter introduced a reporter stationed at the Dallas Police Headquarters that was talking about the transfer of Oswald to the Dallas County Jail. I watched as detectives dressed in business suits came into view escorting Oswald through a gray concrete walled area crowded with reporters. Suddenly a man, later identified as Jack Ruby, lunged from the crowd of reporters, positioned a revolver in Oswald's stomach area and shot him! Oswald audibly moaned as detectives surrounded Ruby. I yelled, "Dad! They just shot Oswald!" Dad came back to the living room with his coffee. He was quiet. I think the whole nation was. No one had ever experienced recent events as traumatic broadcasted live, world wide!

School was cancelled Monday for President Kennedy's funeral. His casket was moved from the East Room at the

White House to the Capital for public viewing Sunday and to the St. Matthews Cathedral Monday for Requiem Mass. I watched as the Presidents casket was placed on the caisson to be drawn by horses to Arlington National Cemetery. The muffled cadence of the drums continued while an announcer in a whisper of a voice described what was happening. Tears built and rolled down my face as the beautiful horse passed, lead by a military person with black riding boots reversed in the stirrups, an awakening for me and a nation.

Chapter 10
Invasion

The Athletic Banquet was tonight and I was going to receive a letter in football. I was looking forward to the large blue and white "M" sewn on my leather sleeved letter jacket. I didn't get to play too much because I was only a sophomore, but enough quarters to qualify for my letter. I knew next year would be a different story. I was slated to start as defensive middle line backer.

Tank, the Twins, Terry, Deon, Larry and mine, with many upperclassmen's names were called by the coach. We were presented our letters and the coach said something about each of us. Coach Bennett said, "Bryan isn't very big but, he likes to be in on every tackle. I look for him to be a defensive key next year." I was handed my letter and the assembled crowd applauded as they did for every recipient. Coach Bennett gave a short speech recapping the past season and what he expected next year. He asked Coach Burns if he wanted to add anything and he said, "I would like to thank the players and the fans and I'm looking forward to next year." Coach Bennett then said, "This concludes tonight's program." As we were leaving Tank and his parents were ahead of us heading for the gymnasium exit and I smiled at him bringing two fingers to my brow similar to a salute. Tank walking behind his parents lowered himself to a semi-squat and duck walked through the doors. It was very funny but Mom or Dad didn't seam to appreciate Tank's ability to entertain like I or my fellow team mates did, although Mom did make a comment to dad about it, "Dale, I wonder what's wrong with him?" That made it all the more funny and I was laughing out loud when Dad turned and gave me a look of distain for Mom's benefit followed by the slyest smile before he turned back to Mom and said, "It doesn't take much to amuse Hoss." I knew he thought Tank's duck walk was funny too, just not as much as I did.

Mrs. Harden traditionally gave an assignment each year to her sophomore English class to establish a pen pal. This may have been one English assignment that aroused my excitement. Finally the day came. It was just before Christmas vacation. Everyone noisily filed into the classroom and took their assigned seats. She sat behind her desk waiting for us to become quiet. Christine placed her finger on her lips and made a 'shhhh' and Mrs. Harden slapped the desk top with a ruler. It became instantly quiet. All we heard was the noise of the steam hissing from a chrome valve on the end of a radiator and some girl coughed. Mrs. Harden didn't say anything for a moment. Finally she rose and said, "This is the way it is to be when you take your seats in this classroom." She was a veteran teacher and we knew she meant exactly what she said. She patted her hand with the ruler and said, "I have an assignment for you over the Christmas vacation." Some classmates casually responded with an 'augh' but a final slap of her palm hushed the room again. She laid the ruler on the desk and picked up a shoe box. Holding the box she said, "This box contains addresses of students, your age, located around the world that would like to have pen pals. I will allow each one of you to select a pen pal. Your assignment is to write this boy or girl a letter and post it over the holidays. Some of you may receive replies before school resumes. I want you to bring them to class and you may be chosen to read the letters out loud in class. As others receive letters I would like for you also to bring them to class. Everyone will have a chance to read a portion of his or her letter in class. I will now allow you to select one address." Mrs. Harden handed the shoe box to Donna and she took a folded piece of paper from the box with a name and address neatly printed on it and passed the box to Janice sitting beside her. The box slowly made its way to me and I selected one from England, it said Great Britain. As I looked at the paper it dawned on me that it was the address of a girl, Linda Gatsby. Linda Gatsby, 2010 West Garden Lane, Liverpool, England, Great Britain was to be my pen pal. I refolded the address using the same creases and carefully put it in my shirt pocket but as I did Mrs. Harden said, "Class I would like for everyone to tell us whom they have selected and what country they live in starting with Donna."

School was going to dismiss early today. The basketball game was away. I wasn't sure what I wanted to do tonight. I did know I wanted to compose a letter to Linda before school was out but I had science next hour and I knew I wouldn't have time and besides Mr. Topping liked to walk up and down the aisles while he lectured. It would be risky to do it in Science class. School was to dismiss after sixth period so I thought unless something came up I would write a letter tonight and I could go to the post office in the morning to mail it.

Upstairs, in my room, I carefully snapped open the note book binder rings and removed a light blue lined, fine red line margined piece of paper and sat down at my desk. It was a small desk that belonged to my grandmother. I was especially fond of her. She was more a friend first and grandmother second. I spent a lot of time with her when I was younger. Grandma, as I called her, taught me much. She always had time for me.

Grandma lived close to us and had a lovely flower garden. I was always impressed in her selection of flowers and their arrangement in her garden. She had small violets in front and tall cannas in the rear with a winding path through the center. She pointed out a line of red ants marching in a line across the path one day. Every other one, it seemed like, had a small green piece of plant life in its pinchers. Some were going one direction and others the opposite. Grandma knelt with me and as we watched, she explained to me how those with the small piece of leaf were going to their home to store the food while others were headed back for more. I ask her about the ones going in the direction of the ones that had a leaf but didn't have one. Grandma said, "They are like people, some have leaves and some don't." I ask, "Why Grandma?" She said, "That's the way God planned it, the ants that are not carrying a leaf are helpers for the ones that are."

I positioned the note book paper on the desk and smoothed it out with the side of my arm. I wrote, "Dear Linda, My name is Bryan and I would like for you to be my pen pal." I went on to tell her where I lived and my age. I heard Dad speak to Mom when he entered the kitchen upon arriving home from work. I ran down the stairs and into the kitchen. My brother was playing with a sock monkey. Anson and that monkey were inseparable. He would fight to the end if he thought for an instant that his prize monkey was in jeopardy. Dad said, "Hoss, I brought something home for you." I said, "What Dad?"

He said, "It's out in the back room." I quickly maneuvered around Mom and through the doorway into the back room. It was a guitar! I picked it up and took it to Dad and said, "Play it Dad!" He said, "After supper Hoss." I took the J-40 Gibson hollow body into the living room and experimented. Soon mom said, "Supper is about ready! Wash your hands." I laid the guitar against Dad's chair hoping it would be the first thing he would see after supper. I joined my family at the table and quickly ate. I was in a hurry to hear Dad play the guitar. I never knew he played; I just took for granted he could. I was surprised to see that everyone else had just gotten a good start so I thought I should not ask to be excused just yet. Then, like a gift from above my little sister, Darlene who had graduated to sitting on a normal chair with a JC Penny and Sears catalog placed on the seat coughed. The cough drew my attention because it was not much more than a whisper. Then without any other notice Darlene vomited on the table and on her self. Everyone eased back from the table but Mom who instantly responded with her apron. Dad responded with an "Ah Balls!" I saw Mom give him a stare as she wiped my sister's face and if I wasn't mistaken detected an ember in the corner of her right eye. Andy stared to cry and Mom said, "Dale, you could do something!" He got up and went to the sink, dampened a wash rag and turned to hand it to my mother. I made my way to the living room.

Dad was close behind me. I had the Gibson holding it out to him and he said nothing as he made his way to the television. He reached down and turned it on and took his usual place. I knew enough to 'let a dead dog lie' so I sat down on the couch beside his chair and experimented with the instrument. Soon the news was over and Dad said, "Let me see that Hoss." I handed the guitar to him.

I watched carefully as he placed his index finger of his left hand on a string and played the string next to it. He then twisted a key on the top of the neck and adjusted the tone of the string so it was close to the pitch of the string he was holding down. I expected a song and ask, "What are you doing Dad?" He said, "Watch, this is the way you tune a guitar." I watched very carefully as he tuned the Gibson. He finished the sixth string and placed three of his fingers of his left hand on strings and strummed the guitar with his right. He returned to tuning. After he was satisfied with the sound he positioned himself on the edge of the chair and played and sang, "You are my sunshine, my only sunshine. You make me happy…" and on the song went. I was amazed! He finished and handed the guitar to me. I took it to the back room and tried to copy what I had seen.

It was morning and I had forgotten about the letter to Linda. I needed to finish it and go up town to the post office. I added to the letter that I hoped to hear from her soon. I inserted it in an envelope and sealed it. I went downstairs and drank a glass of chocolate milk. I told mom what I was up to and left on my bicycle. There had been a light rain sometime last night the streets had puddles. I had to be careful because I had no fenders on my bike and if I rode through a puddle of water the tires would sling water on my back and on the front of my legs and feet. I was almost forced to ride through one because I met a car but was able to slow down enough so the car passed and I swerved around the water. I arrived at the Post Office and Doug's dad met me at the window. He asks me what I needed and I gave him the letter addressed to Linda. Before he said anything else he looked at the letter and said, "England, Doug's pen pal letter was going to Canada. England will cost you more." I watched him over the counter as he checked the postage due for a first class letter to England. He put the book back under the counter and said, "That will be seventeen cents." I gave him two dimes. He thanked me and gave me three cents change. I left the important letter with him.

I rode the half block to Main Street and turned east and just as I did, I saw Billy and Gaiter in front of Hawk Eyes. They didn't see me and went into the pool room. I crossed the street and leaned my bike against the building and went in. I wanted to tell them about the guitar. Both were at the pinball machine which sat in the front of the building. I walked up as Billy was putting in a nickel. Gaiter had already put his in because the number two lit up next to the opening where the score was on the back glass. Gaiter said, "Hi Hoss, you want to play?" I said no because I wanted to get home to practice on the guitar although I sure wanted to take the time to tell them both what I had. I said with excitement, "Guys, guess what I have!" Billy shrugged and Gaiter said, "What? What have you got now?" I answered, "A guitar!" Billy acted unconcerned because he could take or leave music, but Gaiter was excited almost as much as I was. He said, "Hoss, will you show it to me after lunch?" I said, "Sure, come to my house right after lunch." I left and rode slowly on the sidewalk past the Highway Café and looked through the window to see who was there. I didn't see anyone that I wanted to tell about the guitar. As I pulled away from the Highway Café the thought of Rose Ann passed through my mind. I hadn't thought about her for some time but looking through the window of the Highway reminded me of the evening, after the basketball game last year, when I snubbed her when she came inside. I made my way down to the corner and crossed Main Street and noticed the Zenith TV store had a sign in the window stating that they were going out of business. The store was having a sale all next week. I wanted a transistor radio for Christmas and had mentioned it to mom. I'd make sure she knows about the sale when I get home.

Gaiter came over soon after lunch. I already had the guitar out and was practicing on tuning it and heard a noise at the door. It was him. I waved him in and he sat beside me on the floor of the back room. I ask him if he wanted to try it and he held out his arms. I handed the instrument to Gaiter. I noticed that he had an appreciation for it like I did. He held it like a mother would hold a new born baby. Gaiter positioned the guitar on his lap and strummed the stings. He looked at me and smiled. We both took turns for about an hour on it and then decided to go up town. It was Saturday and we wanted to be at Murph's by two o'clock, the time of the Drawing.

I told Mom that we were leaving. It was a cool day but the sun was shining. We rode our bikes past the haunted house without slowing down until we reached the alley by the Post Office that ran parallel with Main Street. We headed down the alley to Murphs and pulled around to the front of the store to lean our bikes just below the plate glass window. There were racks with bread and chips in front of the window but we still could see our bikes. It was always a good idea to keep them in sight because some of the older guys wearing black engineer boots liked to take them around back and lift them up on the low roof covering the rear of the store where the compressors were. We both got a Coke out of the cooler that had cold water circulating around the bottles to cool them and Murph ask if we were going to drink them there. We both said yes, therefore we didn't need to make a deposit for the bottles. Murph always asks, "Are you going to drink it here?"

Gaiter and I talked about the guitar and he said he was going to ask his mom for one. Gaiter's mom was a very gifted person regarding music. She had won a piano in a state competition, which set in their living room. I had never heard her play it but I had heard several people say she was a very good pianist and was quite talented on many other instruments. Considering her background, I assumed it would just be a short time until Gaiter had a guitar. I told him I had listened to an Everly Brother's record and had been trying to play along with it. I had a small record player that was about four inches high with the lid opened and about one foot square. The speaker was very small so the sound was tinny. That made it more difficult to hear the music I wanted to imitate.

Guys started to gather around Murph's counter because it was almost two o'clock. He reached to the side of the old cash register to retrieve the envelope that was stored between the loose side panel and main body of the old machine. The electric Dr. Pepper clock's second hand passed the twelve and Murph carefully tore a narrow strip from the end of the envelope. I think he intentionally took his time to intensify the moment, and removed the card with a name printed on it. Murph picked up his reading glasses that had the left earpiece missing and held them on his nose and red the name, "Violet Porter." Neither Gaiter nor I knew Violet Porter and I didn't hear anyone else mention anything about Porters' either.

Gaiter and I left Murphs and rode on the sidewalk down Main Street. The bakery smelled extra good for that late in the day. I thought about stopping in the drug store to check out the magazine rack and pull the brass arm out on the cigar lighter but we rode on. On the ride home the conversation went back to guitars, music, and Gaiter's plans to positively influence his mom to purchase a six string for him. He was very optimistic that she would buy one, and I was sure hoping Gaiter was right! We decided to get together at his house tomorrow afternoon to practice. I was going to bring the Everly Brother's record and Gaiter said he would check out their record player because he couldn't remember the last time anyone played it. I rode my bike close to my back door as Gaiter continued to his house. It was good to feel the warm back room.

We had an enjoyable Christmas and I received a transistor radio but not the Zenith that was on sale. I got a less expensive one that didn't have a leather case but it received WLS really good at night. That was important because WLS played the latest songs. I dreaded going back to school but tomorrow was the day. Everybody would return with stories about their Christmas Holiday and the girls would act silly about some guy they saw while with their mother shopping or a new record they had. I wanted to look around for someone who might want to join up with Gaiter and me and play music. I had discussed this with Gaiter and he was in favor of the idea. I had two people in mind, Steve and TC. Steve could play the drums and I heard TC could sing *The House of the Rising Sun*. I saw TC during lunch hour being reprimanded by Mr. Tucker. When the principal left TC, I waited a few minutes to make sure he was not overly angry and walked over to the end of the bleachers where he was and made some small talk. I ask TC what Mr. Tucker wanted and he said, "Ah, he was telling me to get my shirt tail tucked in." I saw that he wasn't really upset about the encounter with the principal so I said, "Hey, TC, I heard someone say, they heard you singing *Rising Sun.*" TC looking surprised said, "Who told you that?" I said, "Your sister was telling Katie in English class." TC looked disgusted about his sister talking about him singing. I said, "Wait, I think it is cool! How would you like to come over to Gaiter's tonight and we'll try to play your song." He said, "Ok, what time?" I told him around six or so, started to walk away and turned and said, "I'll see you tonight." I saw Huck standing against the wall watching the girls dance and I joined him just as the first bell rang. We went to the aisle behind the bleachers checking, making sure there were no upper classmen planning an ambush, walked down to our lockers and struggled with the combination padlocks in the dim light. We got our books and Huck and I headed for English Class. Mrs. Harden welcomed us back from vacation then asked if anyone had received a letter back from their prospective pen pals. Christine waved her hand like she was swatting at gnats and Mrs. Harden said, "Yes Christine, would you like to tell us your pen pal's name and where they are from?" Christine said, "Thank you Mrs. Harden, My pen pal's name is Juanita and she lives in Mexico City, Mexico." "Do you have the letter with you today?" Mrs. Harden inquired, and thankfully, Christine didn't. In the weeks to follow many letters were being received by classmates from many interesting places around the world, but some of us hadn't received one yet. That afternoon, after school, I stopped by the Post Office and looked through the small glass on the front of box 465. There was some mail in the box so I worked the combination and removed a city utility bill postcard and a letter with red and blue hash marks around the edge of the envelope. I turned the envelope over and it was addressed to me and from England! I quickly left the inside of the Post Office for some privacy. I carefully opened the envelope making sure not to damage the stamp and unfolded the letter. "Dear Bryan," it read, "It was so good to receive your post." (I guessed this meant my letter.) "I like music and growing flowers in our flower bed. What music do you like? Have you listened to a group called the Beatles? Please tell me more about yourself. I will send you a picture of myself soon. Please send me a picture of yourself. Sincerely, Linda".

I was about half way to the haunted house and pulled the letter from safe keeping, and read it again. I couldn't wait to get a picture from Linda. Soon I was home and Mom was at the kitchen stove replacing a lid on a large pot. I ask, "What you cooking Mom?" She said, "I'm making chili for tonight. You and Anson like chili, and your Dad does too." "I know I do, Mom! Look what I got." I handed her the letter. She looked at the envelope and smiled and started to hand it back. I quickly said, "Mom, you can read it." She replied, "OK, if you would like for me to. Just a minute, let me sit down." She sat at the kitchen table and removed the letter from the envelope. Mom slowly read the letter, folded it with care, inserted it in the envelope and smiled, handing it back to me.

After supper I took the guitar over to Gaiter's and TC was already there. Gaiter's mom had just returned from Terre Haute with a new Gibson ES-175T with a Bigsby tail piece. It was a beautiful red color. Gibson called it wine red. It was a wonderful guitar. At that moment I knew that we were on to something. Gaiter was in the process of tuning the big red guitar so I checked mine with his. I only knew three chords, C, F, and G but I was working on E and A. I told Gaiter that I would play rhythm and he could play lead. I knew Gaiter had much more natural musical talent than most, and it wouldn't take long for him to play lead. I also knew that in the near future I would need to come up with an electric guitar and amp myself. The guitar dad gave me was a very good guitar but I was going to need an electric. I ask Gaiter if he knew *Cathy's Clown* and he said I think I can play it. Well as it turned out neither one of us could play it correctly but that didn't detour TC. Regardless of what chord we strummed he sang it in his key. He was deaf to our guitars! I thought, at the time, that it was ok because neither Gaiter nor I could sing well and we both had our hands full trying to learn to play our guitars. We went over *Cathy's Clown* about five times with TC and then Gaiter and I started to experiment instrumentally. We never played *House of the Rising Sun* that evening. Our finger tips were not callused yet and we both decided to quit for the night. I told TC that we would keep in touch but at the present it was more important for Gaiter and me to become more familiar with our guitars and learn some more chords. TC was ok with that. I think he knew he was limited vocally and he needed to improve also. TC left and we discussed him. I brought up the idea of cleaning out the room in the barn for practice. In the front of the barn behind Gaiter's house was a room finished out which had been used for a craft room or something in the past. He agreed with me so we planned to clean it up the next evening. I also mentioned that a group I had heard about from England was going to be on Ed Sullivan Sunday night. I suggested to Gaiter to be sure and watch. I told him my English pen pal had told me about them some time ago and said they were very good. We planned to work on the practice room the next night.

After supper I went over to Gaiter's to work on the room out in the barn. Gaiter was already out there practicing. He had the room emptied of non-useable things and had some extension cords, two chairs, and an ash tray setting on top of his amp. I was glad that he had the room cleaned up and took my guitar from its case and said, "Let's tune up." With some effort, we tuned together

and when it sounded ok Gaiter said, "Have you heard the
Ventures?" I answered no and Gaiter explained they were
an instrumental group and he liked their music. I ask
him what they played and he said, *Walk, Don't Run.* "Oh,"
I said, "I meant what instruments do they play?" Gaiter
said, "They are a guitar combo, lead, rhythm, bass, and
drums." I ask, "Do you have a record?" Gaiter replied,
"I asked Mom to look at Pages while she is at Terre
Haute and she should be home any time." I noticed he
had brought out his record player and an old end table
which the player was setting on. Gaiter then said, "It
goes like this," and started playing his wine red Gibson.
Gaiter had progressed overnight! He skillfully picked out
the lead of the song, stopped and said, "Your part goes
like this," and played the complementing rhythm part. I
asked him to show me again and went over and over it
while he worked on the lead part. He finally said, "Lets
try it, you ready?" I said, "I may be able to do some of it."
Just then we saw lights of his mom's Pontiac pull into the
drive. Gaiter quickly turned off his amp, laid the neck of
his Gibson on the top of the amp while setting the guitar's
body on a throw rug he had placed on the floor for that
purpose. Gaiter said, "I'm going to find out if she got that
record!" He returned with a LP which he immediately
removed from the cellophane and the record from the
sleeve. While he was doing this I turned on the record
player. Gaiter placed the record on the turntable and after
a few manual oscillations the record found the spindle and
dropped onto the brown felt-covered surface. The turntable was on 45 RPM speed and Gaiter positioned the
speed selector on 33 1/3 RPM, lifted the tone arm and
gently rubbed his index finger over the needle making a
low pitched scratchy sound. He placed the tone arm over
the edge of the record and gently let go of it. Quickly the

needle dropped into the groove on the record surface, and the title song started, *Walk, Don't Run*. We both sat listening intensely to the Ventures. Side one finished and Gaiter said, "Let's listen to the first song again," And repositioned the tone arm. That night we developed our standard for learning new songs.

The week passed quickly and it was Saturday. I asked Gaiter about going uptown. He said he wanted to practice so I told him maybe I'll see him later. I went uptown by myself and met Tank at Murph's. It was just past one o'clock and we had plenty of time before the Drawing. I ask Tank if he had seen Steve and he said no. I told Tank I was gong to run up to the Highway Café to see if Steve was there. He asks, "Why do you need to see Steve?" I replied, "Well, I heard he could play the drums." Tank didn't know what I was talking about, and I left him wondering as I hopped on my bike and rode towards Main Street. I crossed the street and turned right, riding fast on the sidewalk towards the restaurant. Steve usually wasn't in the Highway on Saturday's, only after games on Friday nights. I stopped in front of the restaurant, placing my left foot on the cement that was about six inches high and stuck out below the plate glass window onto the sidewalk. I looked inside and did not see Steve so I rode across the street in front of the drug store. It wasn't long and I was back at Murphs. Billy was there, but he said he was going to Hawk Eyes. I ask him as he pulled up his pedal with his right toe, "If you see Steve, tell him I'm looking for him." Billy took off on his bike, turned and said, "I'll tell him."

I had just enough money for a Coke if I drank it there so I pulled one from the cool water in the red cooler and sat it on the counter. Murph asked his normal question, "Are you..." but I interrupted him and said "Yep," and handed him his money for a 'drink it here'. I walked over to Tank, he was talking to Bob who I hadn't seen enter the store. I told him hello and ask if he had been up to anything. Bob replied, "Nothing you wouldn't do!" We all laughed. It was close to two o'clock, time for the Drawing. We became quiet so we could hear Murph as he opened the envelope and announced the winner. He read off the name of Mable Lowe. We looked at one another, shrugged and I finished the last sip of Coke, placed the bottle in the wooden case setting on the floor making sure Murph noticed me doing so. I told the guys I had to leave and headed for Gaiter's.

Gaiter was in the barn playing along with the Venture record. I entered and listened to Gaiter play, he was doing very well with another song on the album. When he was done I told him I'd be back with my guitar and we would practice. I rode my bike home and walked back to Gaiter's with my guitar. Gaiter wanted me to listen to the new Venture song "*Bull Dog.*" He positioned the tone arm over the correct track and I listened. After the song was finished Gaiter said as he picked up his guitar, "Your part will go like this," as he played the rhythm part. I watched and listened before I tried it. After a few practice run throughs Gaiter said, "Let's try it." We played what would become our signature song for the first time. I was amazed how well Gaiter was playing *Bull Dog.* We practiced for some time and I was getting hungry so I decided to go home. Gaiter said as I was going out the door, "Don't forget that group will be on Ed Sullivan tomorrow night." I almost asked, what group, and then I remembered the Beatles. The group my pen pal told me about and the group the girls at school had began talking about. I turned and told Gaiter, "OK, I'll be sure and watch."

Mom was making potato soup and I was ready to eat! I ask her, "How long until supper Mom?" Mom replied,

"About twenty minutes, go wash your hands." After washing up, I went into the living room where Dad was watching television. "What's on tonight?" I asked. Dad said there was a boxing match on tonight. Dad liked all sports. I said, "Good, what time?" Dad said, "Eight." The news was coming on and I laid down in front of the set, and listened as a reporter talked about some conflict in a place called Vietnam. I remember our civic teacher saying something about Vietnam. Something like, "You people may want to take note of an article found on page twenty three this week. It's entitled, *More Advisors Requested in Vietnam.*" Our civic class used *Newsweek* for our text book. Neither I nor many others in the class paid much attention to Mr. Adams that day. I rolled over and asked Dad, "Dad, where is Vietnam?" Dad said, "In South-East Asia." There was a tone in his voice that caught my attention but I let it pass as Mom said, "Dale, kids, supper is ready."

Sunday started with pancakes. Also sometime last night it had snowed and gotten much colder. I was planning on going over to Gaiter's after lunch to practice but all we had in the Barn, our practice room, was a very small unvented gas space heater and it was cold in there yesterday when it was about forty degrees outside. Today it was in the mid-twenties. I thought I would call Steve after lunch. He probably went to Sunday school. Mom didn't mention Sunday school today, maybe because of the weather. After I removed the sticky syrup from my hands I went upstairs to my room and listened to records and practiced my guitar. I heard the telephone ring and Mom answered it then laid down the receiver, walked over to the register in the dining room ceiling and said, "Bryan, Gaiter is on the telephone and wants to speak to you." I placed the Gibson on my bed and ran down the stairs to the phone. "Hello, what's up?" I said short of breath. Gaiter asks, "Are you going to practice today?" I said, I had been going over some records and he interrupted, "Mom went to Terre Haute so why don't you come over and we can work on our songs?" I said, "I'll be over in a while." We both hung up and I could hear the sizzle of frying and the smell of mom's fried chicken. I went into the kitchen and ask her how long before lunch and she said, with a smile on her face, "Are you hungry already?" I smiled and said, "I'm always hungry for your fried chicken!" Mom's fried chicken also meant mashed potatoes, gravy, rolls, and today, green beans. Soon we sat down and ate. I ask to be excused and also ask, "Will it be all right if I go over to Gaiter's for a while to practice?" Mom said, "OK, but I want you home in an hour or so. You have been spending a lot of time over there." I gave her the old shoulder shrug and look as if I didn't know what she meant and held short of saying anything but, "Ok, I'll be sure and not stay long," knowing full well I would stay most of the afternoon. On the way to Gaiter's I remembered the Ed Sullivan Show and thought more seriously about my length of stay. I didn't want to jeopardize my viewing of the Beatles!

I kicked the snow off my shoes at Gaiter's front door and let myself in. He was sitting on a chair in front of the door playing his Gibson. Each day I was impressed with his improvement. He was doing very well playing the instrumental songs of the Ventures. I wanted to expand to some other songs and mentioned some and he said, "Who are we going to get to sing?" I remembered Steve and ask Gaiter, "Can I use the phone?" Gaiter nodded, and I ask for a telephone book. He asks, "Who are you calling?" I replied, "Steve, where's the phone book?" Gaiter pointed to the telephone directory and I looked up Steve's dad's name, Kenneth. I dialed the number and a woman's voice answered the phone. I figured it was Steve's mom so I used my most polite voice and ask, "May I speak with Steve?" She replied, "May I ask who is calling?" I told her Bryan and she said, "Just a moment," and I heard the receiver being placed on some kind of hard surface. It was unusually quiet in the background and seemed like a long time before Steve picked up the phone saying hello. The way Steve said hello, rather reserved, influenced me to wait until Monday at school before I actually ask him about playing the drums so I told him I would like to talk with him tomorrow before class. We agreed to meet at the end of the bleachers in the old gym, the end close to the boy's restroom. I thanked him and said, "I'll see you in the morning." Steve hung up without saying anything. I told Gaiter about the conversation and also expressed my concern about Steve. I thought he may not show tomorrow. Soon Gaiter and I were playing together and I was consumed with learning enough to keep up with him. The afternoon soon turned gray as the sun disappeared behind Billy's house across the street. I had lost track of time and as fast as I could get my guitar in its case I told Gaiter I'd see him tomorrow and rushed out his door and across the street home.

I entered the back door quietly hoping not to arouse anyone because I had spent so much time at Gaiter's. I thought the best place to be was upstairs so as I walked with as much stealth as I cold muster through the kitchen and entered the dining room, Anson, who was playing with some Lincoln Logs on the floor loudly announced, "Hoss is home!" So I changed my plan and entered the living room asking mom, "Mom, what's for supper?" She looked up from her *Ladies Home Journal* and didn't answer my question but asked, "What were you doing at Gaiter's for so long?" I smiled and said, "We were practicing

Mom, what's for supper?" If I could only get her to drop the query about being gone all afternoon and answer my question, "What's for supper?" Finally she said, "I'm planning on leftovers." I was successful!

After supper my brother and I took a bath together and my mom bathed my sister. I took my place on the floor in front of the television and Anson was on the couch with his sock monkey and Freckles. Mom and my sister were doing something in the kitchen. I think Mom was mending something because I noticed she had the round, gray tin box that has white cattails and a white bird painted on the lid lying on the kitchen table. This round box contained bits of cloth, thread, assorted zippers, and needles. Many of the items had been in the box for as long as I could remember. Sewing wasn't one of Mom's favorite things to do. I was getting anxious for the show to start. It felt like hours had passed then after a commercial, the familiar opening, the announcer said, "And now, here is Ed Sullivan!" Ed walked to center stage while the audience applauded and responded, "Thank you very much. Now yesterday and today our theater has been jammed with newspaper reporters and hundreds of photographers from all over the nation, and these veterans agree with me that the city has never experienced the excitement stirred by these youngsters from Liverpool who call themselves the Beatles. Now tonight, you are twice going to be entertained by them, right now and in the second half of our show. Now, ladies and gentlemen, the Beatles!" The people in the theater were screaming with excitement as the Beatles opened with, "Close your eyes and I'll kiss you, tomorrow I'll miss you...." They had something that was very difficult to explain, but immediately I knew without a doubt, that I wanted it too! Our culture had been invaded by four guys from England.

Chapter 11
The Silhouettes

Monday morning, before the first bell, I looked for Steve
at the end of the bleachers by the boy's restroom. I thought
he had forgotten but just then he came down the stairs,
skipping every other step. Steve said, "Hi Bryan, sorry
I'm a little late. It's about time for the first bell!" I said, "I
know, so I'll get right to it. Would you like to join Gaiter
and me at a practice this week? We are starting a group."
He replied, "What kind of group?" I felt foolish, being
evasive on what I wanted, but I was afraid he would say
no. I needed to buy some time so I ask him if he had seen
the Beatles on Ed Sullivan last night. Steve answered yes
and seemed somewhat excited. Maybe it was because the
school was buzzing about them, I don't know, but he did
seem honestly excited. Now was the time, "Steve, would
you like to play the drums in a group some of us are
starting?" He ask, "Who?" I was hesitant to tell him it
was just Gaiter and I. I answered, "Well I'm just looking
for some guys now, nothing permanent." He said as the
first bell rang, "We'll talk some more later, we need to
get to class."

It had been a long morning and I spent a lot of time

day-dreaming of spring and who may be good at playing bass. Gaiter and I needed a drummer and a bass player to make up the combo. The bell, it was lunch break. I raced Huck down the two flights of stairs and behind the bleachers. We haphazardly stored our books in our lockers and made our way to the school cafeteria for lunch. As we reached the landing and doors that lead to the new gym and cafeteria we were engulfed by an odor, an odor of floor wax, pine trees, and vomit. Someone had up-chucked and all the custodian had accomplished was sprinkle some of that stuff that looked like sawdust and came in a sack like coffee in the area. The rush of traffic across the landing and through the doors made for an unpleasant situation as we lined up to be served our lunch. Huck pointed and said, "Look at that!" as Linda broke ranks and ran towards the girls' restroom with her hands covering her mouth. The odor had claimed another student. Huck said, "I hope she makes it!" After eating we left the new gym and returned to the old building.

The girls were dancing in front of the stage as the phonograph played *Peggy Sue*. Just before the song ended Christine approached three other girls standing close to the record player. She opened a pink folder and they all started screaming. The record had just stopped and many others gathered around and they too started screaming. Huck and I looked at each other expressing wonderment. What could be going on? As we looked around there were two distinct groups, either those who were wondering, like Huck and I, and those screaming on the gymnasium floor. TC had been sitting on the stage close to the record player. Tank and Bob were leaning against the large protective pad that hang on the wall behind the basketball backboard and one of them must of waved TC over to ask him what was happening. Huck and I joined Tank and

Bob. TC came over and Tank asked, "What's wrong with those stupid girls?" TC replied, "Christine has a picture of the Beatles." Tank said, "Those girls are nuts!" The first bell rang and we all went to our lockers to pick up our books for class.

Gaiter and I met at the barn after school and I ask him if he saw the girls at noon hour. He looked puzzled so I told him about all the screaming over the picture Christine had. Gaiter shook his head from side to side and said, "Let's practice." We played the two Venture songs and I suggested a song entitled *Let's Go*. He asked how it went and I crudely played some of it. Gaiter remembered it and quickly was playing it quite well. Between songs I brought up Steve. I told Gaiter that he hadn't said anything more to me about playing the drums. Gaiter suggested asking him again, he said, "We don't have anything to lose." It was getting dark and time to call our session quits for now. I put my old Gibson in its battered case and left for home.

There was a home basketball game Friday. I knew Huck planned on going as well as I did. Friday night we met before the game in the cafeteria area because it was very cold outside. They folded the tables into the walls and stored the chairs making room for concessions. The popcorn smelled extra good tonight although I was saving my money for a chocolate shake at the Highway Café after the game. We lost the game. The only notable excitement was when our coach was ejected from the game for throwing a towel onto the playing floor. A referee made a call that Coach didn't agree with. His temper escalated as he took several steps towards the referee. He was yelling and flailing his arms and the official called a technical foul on him. That only escalated the situation and Coach threw a towel towards the referee and the official immediately ejected the coach. The visitors were certainly pleased and the Big Blue's fans displayed their support for our coach with robust boos. Huck and I walked into the cafeteria with four minutes and six seconds left in the game. Tank and Bob were just about to go out the door and we joined them. We were chilled to the bone by the time we reached the Highway Café. We got the first four stools at the counter and Crutchy ask us what we would like. Huck ordered a chocolate shake, Tank a vanilla, Bob ordered a cherry Coke and I a chocolate shake. As Crutchy scooped the ice cream into the stainless steel containers and added the other ingredients Bob demonstrated a new trick he learned. We all watched intently as Bob dispensed a small amount of salt from the shaker onto the counter top. Using his index finger he carefully positioned the salt into a very small compact pile. Leaning back as to inspect the small deposit on the worn counter top he removed a nickel from his jean pocket and laid it beside the salt. Crutchy placed the red plastic glass containing Bob's cherry Coke on the counter. Bob looked to his right where Tank was sitting and then to his left where Huck and I were then picked up the glass with one hand and grasped the straw with the other placing it between his lips taking a swig. Bob then picked up the nickel and slowly placed it on edge, leaning it sideways, in the salt. It appeared the coin was setting on edge, leaning over somewhat. We all gave Bob a that-a-boy and proceeded to duplicate the trick ourselves, at least Huck and I did. Tank said, "I saw TC do that the other day."

People started arriving and taking the available seats. Crutchy and his helper became very busy as the restaurant filled to capacity. The Playhouse had closed the first of February and those customers naturally came to the Highway making it more crowded than usual. Huck suggested that we go to Hawk Eyes and play the pinball machine. So we left the restaurant and walked the short walk west a few doors to the pool hall. Hawk Eye gave us a nod when we entered the pool hall and walked over to the pinball machine. It was strange that no one was already playing the machine but it was sitting there begging for a nickel. "Who is playing?" Bob ask. Huck said, "Wait, I want to try something." He walked toward the first table which wasn't being used, checked to make sure Hawk Eye wasn't watching while he removed two pieces of chalk from the table rail. I ask Tank, "What is Huck doing?" Tank said, "Who knows!" Huck nonchalantly returned and handed me one of the cubes of blue pool cue chalk and said, "Tank, you and Bob pick up the front of the machine and Hoss and I will place the chalk under the legs." Tank looked puzzled, but he turned his attention to Hawk Eye waiting for something to distract the manager. It wasn't long, someone had made an opening shot and the cue ball bounced off the table and rolled down the old oiled wood floor, rattled between chair legs before coming to rest. Hawk Eye made it to the second to last table and the guys playing eight ball took note. Nothing was said; Hawk Eye's walk down the room triggered an air of concern among the players. When he turned to walk back to his chair behind the counter the boys smiled at each other as play resumed. It was just enough time for Bob and Tank to lift the front legs up while Huck and I placed the chalk under them. This decreased the slope of the playing surface, which slowed the steel ball considerably, making it much easier to rack-up a high score. Huck cautioned us about using too much "english," the practice of bumping the machine with your palms to hopefully influence the balls path. The increased elevation also increased the sensitivity of the tilt mechanism. Huck and Bob decided to play and Tank and I would keep our feet placed to block Hawk Eyes view of the chalk cubes under the legs. It wasn't long until Huck had accumulated enough points the machine started rewarding him with free games. The loud wooden block click signaled the award. The first two back to back clicks did not arouse Hawk Eye's suspicion but the next three loud clicks in rapid succession did! He was giving us the evil eye just as the machine clicked off two more just as Huck intentionally tilted the machine causing all play to stop and all the lights to go out except the word "Tilt" which was lit up in the lower right corner of the back glass.

We looked at each other waiting for someone to say or do something as Hawk Eye made his way toward us and the machine. Hawk Eye normally carried the large half of a pool cue as a badge of authority. We never saw him hit anyone but it wasn't because he didn't try. We scrambled to get out of his way and he noticed the chalk under the legs. He took the cue and wacked the chalk cubes and the legs until the cubes turned into a blue smudge on the dark oiled floor and the machine was back to its normal level. We all backed away from Hawk Eye, towards the door, and as he turned towards us we made our exit but not before Tank flipped him the bird. All four of us stood outside of the pool room and laughed until our sides hurt. We all decided to go down to Murph's and as we passed the large plate glass window of the Highway Café Tank assumed his duck walk posture. We laughed until we reached the end of the block.

There were a few older guys in Murphs sitting on the boxes of canned vegetables behind the cooler. We waited around for about fifteen cold minutes standing on the sidewalk in front of Murph's waiting and hoping for something exciting to happen without success. It was going to be a long walk home for all of us and Huck would need to go to Tanks to get his bicycle for his ride home. It was good that Tank's house was along the route Huck normally would take. It seemed no one wanted to make the move to leave but we all were hoping someone would break the ice, thus allowing the others to maintain their ego. The waiting game ended when Tank said, "Guys, I'll see you later. Huck, are you going with me?" We departed saying half hearted, "See you later and a see you tomorrow."

Saturday I went over to Gaiter's and found him practicing. I brought my guitar so I joined him. After a few songs, Gaiter ask me if I had talked any more to Steve and I told him I had not seen him but I would call him now. I leaned my guitar against a chair and walked over to the phone. I had forgotten Steve's number so I had to look it up again. Soon I had an answer. It was Steve. "Hello Steve. This is Hoss, Gaiter and I are playing a few songs and wondering if you have made a decision about playing the drums?" Steve said, "Yes, I'll get together with you guys as soon as I can. How about this afternoon, will that be OK?" I replied, "That will be great, about one o'clock at Gaiter's?" "I'll be there at one," Steve said. Gaiter and I were excited about practicing with a drummer and Steve was good.

At lunch I mentioned that I would like to buy a new electric guitar and amp. Dad said I already had a good guitar, which I did but I told him I needed an electric. Dad said, "It's your money." I only had thirty two dollars saved up from last summer's yard mowing. I wasn't sure how much an electric guitar and amp would cost but I did know that the music store in Terre Haute would take a small down payment and monthly installments. The problem, I needed a parent to co-sign the agreement. I dropped the conversation before anyone could say something negative. Mom asked, "Bryan, what are you doing after lunch?" I said, "We got Steve on the phone and he agreed to set in with us this afternoon at one." "Well don't forget you have other things to do, like homework," she said. I replied, "Ok Mom, I'll do homework tonight." Actually I hoped to watch *Have Gun Will Travel* and *Gunsmoke* tonight on television.

I arrived at Gaiter's before one. I wanted to be sure we had an area that Steve could use to set up his drums. We moved the dining room table against the wall and pushed the chairs under the table. This left a small area just large enough, we thought. We had just finished moving the chairs when Gaiter noticed a strange car driving very slowly. He said, "I think Steve is here." I looked just in time to see the top of a bass drum setting on the back seat of the Chevy four-door. Without my coat I went out the front door onto the porch to signal, if need be, that they were at the correct house. Steve saw me and must have said something to his dad because they turned into Gaiter's driveway. I crunched over the frozen snow that had many foot prints embedded before it refroze to help Steve with the drums. He said hello and handed me a collection of what appeared to be chromed pipes of various shapes and sizes. He removed a snare drum that was setting beside the bass drum and we made our way across the crunchy snow. We set the stuff on Gaiter's carpeted floor and Steve said, "I'll get the rest of the stuff, you guys don't have your coats on." Steve made two more trips out returning with a cymbal and bass drum. His father slowly backed out the drive and drove towards town. Steve started to assemble the drum set and spent a lot of time adjusting and repositioning until he had his equipment just right. I said, "Gaiter lets try *Bull Dog*, and

I'll start off with the rhythm lick." Steve came in just as Gaiter started the lead. What a difference drums made! Everything fell into place that Saturday afternoon.

Mr. Stewart heard that we had started a combo and asked if we would like to play a song during the spring band concert. We answered yes. The concert was held during an assembly in the old gym. Usually the principal would say a few words about upcoming events and introduce the music director Mr. Stewart. Over the years Mr. Stewart had developed an outstanding music program. We had a pep band which played during basketball games, the marching band, jazz band, choirs and the Villagers, a singing ensemble. The assembly was scheduled for the second Friday in March which was just around the corner. Steve, Gaiter, and I wondered which song to play and the discussion illuminated the need for a singer. We hadn't given much thought to vocals after we met with TC several weeks ago. Gaiter and I were keeping busy learning Venture instrumental songs. We decided to ask TC to sing with us at the assembly. The only song that I thought he could possibly sing was *The House of the Rising Sun*. I had spent some time working on it by myself and I knew Gaiter and Steve could pick it up easily. The question was would TC do it? We planned on getting together after school to practice and we would talk more about it then.

When I arrived home I called TC's house but he wasn't home. I picked up my guitar and went over to Gaiter's. I called TC's again and while the phone rang, I hoped he would be the one to answer, not his sister Christine. She did. I knew my call would arouse her curiosity because TC and I were friends but never hung around together much. It wasn't that I didn't want people to know about us, I just wanted to do it on our terms. If we couldn't get a good sound by the assembly we could tell Mr. Stewart and he would understand allowing us to cancel without any ramifications. I didn't want our fellow classmates anticipating something that we couldn't pull off!

I asked TC if he would come over to Gaiter's because we wanted to try a new song. He asked, "Now?" and I said, "Yes, I'll fill you in when you get here." He said he would be on his way. It wasn't long before TC arrived. I described the situation regarding the assembly and that I wanted to keep everything under cover at this time. He asked what song did we have in mind and I told him *The House of the Rising Sun*. TC said, "I know that song, let's try it." I told Gaiter that I had worked on it and it started in A minor. I quickly played through the other chords and Gaiter instantly caught on. I ask if everyone was ready and TC stepped into the kitchen and returned with a broom. "What's that for?" Steve asks. TC said, "This is my mic." At that point I knew that we had a lot of ground to cover in a short time. We went through the song and it was weak. Each of us was trying to fit in. By the completion of the third run through it was better. I suggested we play *Bull Dog* and then come back to *The House of the Rising Sun*. We did and the fourth time it was much better. It was close to five o'clock so we decided to break up and come back Thursday. TC said he would work on his part and I cautioned him to remember about keeping things under cover. He said, "Don't worry. I won't do or say anything around Christine."

It was Wednesday, just two days before the assembly when Mr. Stewart stopped me in the hall way. "Excuse me Bryan," he said, "We are preparing a program for the students at the assembly and I forgot to ask you the name of your group and what song you were going to perform?" We had been totally consumed with getting our song presentable that naming the group was never discussed. I felt between a rock and a hard place. I was stalling, trying to think of something to say and Mr. Stewart said, "We need to get the program mimeographed today." The name Viking, Vikings came to mind, so I said, "We call ourselves the Vikings and we'll do *The House of the Rising Sun.*" Mr. Stewart smiled and thanked me. I needed to find Gaiter, Steve and TC and ask everyone to meet after lunch. I decided we would meet on the bleachers. I saw Steve walking towards the math room, stopped him and said we needed to have an emergency meeting after lunch, "Meet on the bleachers, on the east end. If you see Gaiter or TC, be sure to tell them!" Steve asks, "What's going on?" I said, "Nothing bad, I'll tell you when we meet." I saw TC in front of the boy's restroom and ran down there to tell him as the first bell rang. After History class I saw Gaiter and Tom walking towards the Science room and caught up to them just before they entered the door. I told Gaiter about the meeting and he said he would be there.

After leaving the cafeteria I went directly to the old building and to the bleachers. I climbed to the second to top row. Soon I was joined by Steve and TC. We waited for a few minutes and Gaiter didn't appear so I told the guys the situation. That Mr. Stewart asked what song we were going to do and what we called ourselves. He said he was mimeographing a program for Friday and needed the information. I knew I had to tell him something so I told him we called ourselves The Vikings, and we were going to play *The House of the Rising Sun.* Neither Steve nor TC looked angry about the name. I was thankful about that. Steve wondered where Gaiter was and I told him I didn't know although I had told him about the meeting.

I caught up with Gaiter after school. We walked together down the alley towards home. I said, "Did you forget about the meeting?" He said, "No, Tom and I had something to do. What was it about?" I told him, and he wasn't troubled at all about the name, The Vikings. I reminded him about practice Thursday after school and said TC had borrowed a microphone from the AV room and hoped it would work in his amp. He said, "We'll see Thursday."

We gathered at the barn after school Thursday and went through the song four times. The sound wasn't good but I thought it was acceptable. I knew we weren't where I wanted us to be. I laid in my bed going over the song and our parts watching the red light blink on and off on the tower at the tank farm west of town. I did a lot of thinking watching that red light blink. I decided what we needed was to get through the assembly tomorrow and then if things went ok, work on what needed to be done to improve the sound of the band.

We set our stuff up on the gym floor to the left of the stage during lunch hour. We didn't have a sound check. In fact; I don't know if we had ever realized that we should, and don't think it would have improved anything. There was the possibility that it may have revealed just how weak we were and negatively influenced our first performance! We were sitting in seventh hour study hall, I watched the large clock over the study hall monitors desk slowly approach two forty-five. I wasn't nervous; I was anxious, anxious to see if we would be accepted. Finally the principal manually rang the dismissal bell and everybody filed out of the study hall and classrooms. After storing their books, they made their way to the bleachers in the old gym. Steve, Gaiter, TC and I sat on the west end of the bleachers across from our equipment. The Villagers took their places on three portable steps placed in the center of the floor. Mr. Stewart walked across the gym floor to where the Villagers were and turned to face the student body. He said, "Welcome to our spring concert! Today we have a great program for you. First the Villagers will perform two songs, *Oklahoma* from the musical and their second selection will be *Moon River*. And then a special surprise, a new combo, The Vikings will perform *The House of the Rising Sun.*" Amazingly, we heard from behind us, some ooh's and a few claps of applause. "And now the Villagers will sing *Oklahoma*," Mr. Stewart announced. Mr. Stewart turned facing his highly acclaimed group, raised his hands and led the choir in a beautiful rendition of the song. The student body realized that we were fortunate to have a musical director as dedicated as Mr. Stewart and he was well respected by all. The assembled students and teachers gave the Villagers a robust round of applause and when the gym silenced, Mr. Stewart conducted them singing *Moon River*. Again everyone applauded and Steve, Gaiter, TC and I made our way toward our equipment. As the applause subsided and the Villagers took seats in the bleachers, Mr. Stewart said, "Now I'm very pleased to present The Vikings!" The applause and yells were surprising! We were not expecting the reception we were receiving. I waited for the noise to quiet some because I had to start the song by playing the intro, Am, C, D, F, Am, E, Am, E and Steve and Gaiter came in as well as TC singing. The students in the bleachers were screaming. I think they were mimicking what they saw on the TV! It was good too, they couldn't hear our mistakes. We finished the song to a thunderous applause and when the noise subsided they didn't seem too over anxious to leave but Mr. Stewart, raised his voice, thanked them and announced that they were dismissed. We picked up our equipment feeling like successful gladiators returning victorious from a hard fought crusade. I reminded everyone about practice Tuesday after school.

Gaiter and I got together Saturday afternoon and practiced. He or I didn't go up town to the Drawing. It was snowing and there already was five inches on the ground. We talked a lot about Friday and came to the conclusion; the sound we wanted wasn't there. I suggested we talk to Steve and Gaiter agreed. Monday before first class I found Steve and asked him if he could meet with us after lunch and he said ok. I suggested we meet down by the Biology room. After eating a sloppy joe, green beans, fruit cocktail, and a small carton of chocolate milk I left Tank and Huck to meet the guys. We gathered in front of the Biology room and Steve suggested we climb the stairs to the first landing which we did. We ascended the stairs and when we reached the landing I opened the discussion by saying that I felt that "things" were not just right concerning our sound. Gaiter didn't say anything but Steve agreed saying that we were not as tight musically as he wanted. I told him that was a good way to describe it. He also said he would like to try singing. That surprised me! I didn't know Steve could sing. I responded, "That would be great! Do you think you can borrow the microphone TC had borrowed from the AV department?" Gaiter hadn't said anything until he interrupted, "I can get a microphone." "Ok, great Gaiter, let's give it a try Tuesday at practice, and before I forget, how about another name for the group?" I asked. "I'm not happy with the Vikings," I said. Steve said he would think about it and the first bell rang.

That evening I was listening to my transistor radio lying on my bed looking at the red light on the tower blink on and off. Then it came to me, we needed a bass player. Who could we ask? I thought of many guys but could not think of one that I thought would be interested. The more I listened to the radio and watched the light I knew I was on the right track. A bass would fill in the gap in our sound! The unanswered question was our lead vocals. This question might be answered tomorrow night.

The Silhouettes, Hoss, Doug, Kirk, Steve, and Gaiter seated

It was still cold and the snow drifted because of a strong overnight wind. I wondered what effect the cold would have on my old Gibson. It was good to get inside Gaiter's. I had just entered when I saw Steve's dad pull into Gaiter's drive. Steve made two trips bringing in his drum equipment while I tuned up with Gaiter. While Steve was setting up his drums, I asked him if he had thought of any names for us. He said as he was adjusting his kick pedal, "Yes, I have a name in mind. What do you think of The Silhouettes?" "I think it's perfect! What do you think Gaiter?" I asked. Gaiter said, "I think it is good!" Gaiter gave Steve the microphone he had and Steve asked where he got it. Gaiter said he asked his mom to pick one up at the music store. Gaiter also pointed to a microphone stand in the corner. Steve set it up and handed the plug to Gaiter who plugged it into his amp. I suggested we try playing *The House of the Rising Sun*, the only vocal song we all knew. I ask Steve if he knew the words and he said most of them, so I started the song. "The Silhouettes," a good name!

By the end of March we asked Doug if he would like to play bass with us and he agreed. The sound was good. The bass completed our sound for the time being. On March 27th I purchased my new electric guitar and amp. Dad co-signed the promissory note at the music store. We practiced every Tuesday and Thursday in the barn. Doug gave us a bigger gas space heater and we could leave our instruments in the practice room between practices. We all had keys and it wasn't unusual to have impromptu jam sessions on the weekends. During one of these impromptu sessions Gaiter's older brother Johnny met with us and offered his services as our manager. We accepted his offer. He took the role as cheerleader, promoter, big brother, booking agent, and manager.

Billy and I joined Bud for the first show at the drive-in this season. Bud lived a block behind Billy and had his drivers license. The first movie was *Thunder Road* which Billy and I didn't watch much of. We were looking at the girls coming and going at the concession stand. There were yellow bug lights at the four corners of the concession stand and if you were parked in the first or second row behind the stand the dim yellow lights would make it easy to see who went in and out.

We were standing beside Bud's car by the speaker pole listening to the speaker still on the stand. There was no one parked next to the car on the driver's side. Tank had joined us and we were taking particular delight in selecting or rejecting girls who walked into the yellow light. Comments like, "I wouldn't touch her with a ten foot pole," or "she is so hot she could kiss me in broad day light," were handed back and forth with enthusiasm.

On rare occasions the manager of the drive-in would receive a telephone call asking to speak to someone attending the movie. I'm sure he asked if it was an emergency and if he decided it was important he would page whomever over the speaker system. That night, out of the blue, the movie sound track silenced and a scratchy voice called my name and said, "Would you please come to the concession stand for a telephone call!" I had no idea what to expect. I think I was more embarrassed than scared though. I walked just fast enough towards the stand as not to arouse suppression and slowed when I was within the range of the yellow light. I entered the concession stand and told the girl behind the counter that I was paged and had a phone call. She motioned me to the end of the counter and lifted a telephone from under the green formica counter top and set it in front of me, and said, "Be fast." I picked up the receiver that was lying beside the phone and said hello. I heard a voice responding but I couldn't understand what they were saying over the noise of popcorn popping, ice being scooped, customers placing orders, and the sound track of the movie being played on small metal speaker horns located at each side of the room. I said, "I can't hear you." Then I recognized Johnny's voice. He sounded very excited but I needed to ask him to repeat what he had said again. He was telling me that he had booked us (The Silhouettes) at Paris Twin Lakes. We were to play next Saturday night. I said, "But Johnny, we know only four songs!" His reply was, "You guys have a week to get ready." I returned to Bud's car and Billy asks me, "What was that about?" I said, "It was Johnny. He has booked the band at Twin Lakes next Saturday night." Bud had returned to his car when he heard the page thinking he may need to take me home because of an emergency. He said, "Is that all!" I'm sure Billy and Tank felt the same way but neither said anything.

Sunday afternoon I went to the barn. Gaiter was working on the instrumental part in *Louie Louie*. He appeared as always, calm and in deep concentration. I interrupted him and said, "What do you think about Saturday night?" He, as usual, smiled and shrugged his shoulders. I nervously said, "We have only four songs!" "Well I'm working on a song", Gaiter said. I got out my new guitar and asked him how to play my part. Gaiter instructed me how to play it and ask, "Are you ready to try it? You start it like this." He played the intro and when he finished I repeated the intro and he came in. It relieved me some knowing that we could add another song to our list but I knew it was going to take a miracle to play two hours with just five songs! At practice Tuesday night we all decided to practice on Thursday and Friday night too. Gaiter had another new song, an instrumental, called, *Wipe Out*. We worked on it and Steve picked up the drum solo well. We could use it Saturday too. I was optimistic that just maybe, just maybe we could pull it off. Johnny was at all of our practices that week working hard building our confidence. Friday night Johnny suggested that he rent a small U-Haul trailer to move our equipment. We agreed and also agreed to pay him for the U-Haul rental from our profit.

Saturday, Johnny was at the barn at four o'clock with the U-Haul backed close to the practice room. We were all there by four thirty and loaded our instruments into the small trailer. Gaiter's mom had purchased us blue stripped shirts and we all decided to wear black pants. We looked like a 'Group' for the first time. We all rode with

Johnny to Twin Lakes. Johnny spoke with the manager and he showed Johnny where he wanted us to set up. We quickly set our equipment up and noticed a few people watching us from the outside. The Twin Lakes pavilion had panels that swung out, opening up to the outside. These were open and it made us nervous because we were going to run through *Bull Dog*. Johnny could stand in the rear of the pavilion and listen to our sound and critique it so we could make necessary adjustments. Just before we ran through the song, Johnny called us together and gave a pep talk no less as animated as a football coach would make at a state championship game. It was just what we needed. Johnny walked to the rear of the pavilion and gestured for us to play. I started the song playing the hard rhythm introduction and Steve rolled off on the drums as the others joined. Our signature sound was born that late afternoon. We were about half way through *Bull Dog* and Johnny raised his hands and whistled loudly signaling us to stop. He walked back from the rear of the pavilion and said, "Ok boys, this is it. This is what we have been waiting for. Let's walk over to the bench by the trailer and wait until time to play."

We sat watching guys and girls migrate towards the pavilion and pass through the concession area getting their hand stamped when they paid the entry fee. Someone, maybe the manager, turned on the lights, bulbs mounted in porcelain fixtures spaced about eight feet apart on the ceiling and red and blue flood lights that shined on our equipment. "All right boys," Johnny exclaimed, "Let's give it to them!" We quickly and quietly walked through the concession area and around the edge of the dance floor. We nervously donned our guitars as Steve sat on the small stool behind his drums. I took a quick look at Steve and he nodded. I turned facing the crowd and played the starting lick, Steve rolled off with a great drum intro as Gaiter and Doug joined in. The girls on the dance floor screamed and The Silhouettes were to become one of the more popular bands in the area.

Johnny filled the schedule with bookings Friday's and Saturday's that spring and summer. He also booked two homecoming dances in the fall. The hometown kids anxiously awaited us to play in our hometown. Johnny had intentionally booked us away from home for a few weeks to allow us the time to grow, he said. The second Saturday in June we were scheduled to return home, booked to play at the American Legion. We were all excited to play in our hometown. Our friends and classmates not only in M'ville, but surrounding towns were just excited as we were. Most of the girls were following the Beatles, Rolling Stones, and a California group, the Beach Boys very closely. Surprisingly, they would transfer their enthusiasm for the English and American groups to us! The Silhouettes were at the right place at the right time.

My cousin Dave owned a 1948 Dodge four door and he asked me if I wanted to buy it. He said he would sell it to me for thirty-five dollars. I asked Dad if it would be all right and he said ok. So I became a proud owner of a car. I didn't have my driver's license yet but next year I would take driver's training. Dave brought the Dodge over Friday. As soon as he left I pulled the car around beside the garage so the garden hose would reach it and gave it a wash down. I spent the afternoon cleaning the inside while playing the radio.

That evening Gaiter came by and I took him for a ride down the alley. Right away I noticed that the right front brake would lock and not release until the car came to a halt. Dave used the emergency brake. I was wondering why, now I knew. I told Gaiter that I would take the wheel off and take a look at the wheel cylinder and brake shoes next week. We make it back to the backyard. Gaiter said, "The radio sounds good!"

I asked Gaiter if he was going uptown tomorrow for the drawing. He said he didn't know. I was planning on going uptown tonight and maybe catching a ride with someone who had a car. Maybe Beth would be in town. I met Beth at a sock-hop we played at several weeks ago. She had her driver's license and drove a red Ford Falcon.

I met Tank at Murph's, it was just about dark. Tank said, "Are you getting any strange?" I said, "Nope, not yet anyway." We both laughed and walked towards Main Street. Woods, in his fifty-seven black and white Chevy convertible came around the corner and nailed it. He passed Murph's accelerating in second gear and at the welding shop, let off the gas, racking off. His black and white Chevy was the best sounding car in town. Tank said he was going to get a new car when he got his license. I asked Tank if he was coming to the dance tonight and he said yes. I told him we expected a large crowd. We continued to walk towards the middle of the block noticing the vacant building where the Zenith store was and a new vacancy, the bakery had closed. I heard the Ross Shop was closing too. I ask Tank, "Have you heard anything about the Ross Shop?" Tank said, "Yah, they are closing at the end of the month".

We crossed the street in the middle of the block and went in the Highway Café. Peggy and Elaine were sitting at a table with Bubby. They were cheerleaders. Bubby was the only male cheerleader in the area and because of his dedication was well accepted. We sat down at the counter and Tank ordered a cherry Coke and I got a Coke. We were about half finished with our sodas when Bob came in and sat down beside us saying, "Hi fellows!" Bob ordered a

Coke. I ask him, "Are you coming to the dance tonight?" He said he planned on it. I ask him, "What did your mom say about what happened in Industrial Arts Class?" Bob said, "She doesn't know about it," laughing.

Our Industrial Arts teacher was a good guy. We nick-named him Captain Crunch, after a caricature on a serial box that we imagined resembled him. In class Monday we all were working in the shop on our woodworking projects. It was almost time for us to leave the shop area and go to the adjoining classroom and listen to the Captain's lecture on woodworking. Bob crawled inside one of the large work benches and closed the door just as the bell rang. It was a two-period class and we had about five minutes before the last bell. We all, except Bob, picked up our tools and Huck, Wallace, and I went to the back double door. We stepped outside and held the door from closing and locking us outside with a block of wood. We discussed the cars in the student parking lot and counted the cars that had "Cam Busters" signs displayed in the back glass. The warning bell rang and we made our way to the classroom and took our seats. The Captain started talking about the correct method of using dowel joints when we heard a faint baa, like a lamb! It was so faint that the Captain didn't notice, but he did stop suddenly and ask, "Has anyone seen Bob?" We looked as innocent and concerned as we could and then a louder baa came from the shop. We snickered as the Captain made his way to the rear of the classroom and entered the shop. He just stood inside the door when Bob did it again. The Captain eased towards the bench that Bob was hiding in and just as he emitted another baa the Captain opened the door and pulled Bob out from his hiding place. He brought Bob to the classroom by the arm and presented him before the class and said, "Bob is so very talented I'm going to let him spend the rest of today and next week entertaining us!" The Captain instructed Bob to go back to his work bench and crawl under it and baa every thirty seconds. Captain said, "Bob, you do it loud enough that we all can enjoy it!" We all laughed as Bob took the long walk to begin his punishment.

Johnny said we needed to be at the Legion by five-thirty so I told Tank and Bob I would see them tonight. I walked home and took a bath and washed my hair. I combed it in a Beatle style and wondered what it would look like when it dried. Steve and Gaiter also were going to try combing their hair like the Beatles. Doug wouldn't give us an answer and ignored our suggestions about it. We all purchased matching English cut gray sports jackets which sported a black velvet strip on the collar. Steve and I had also purchased Beatle boots. I dressed slowly making sure everything looked as good as it could. I got the thin necktie knot correct on the third attempt. Johnny was going to haul our equipment and asked us to meet him at the barn and help him load it in the U-Haul. I told Mom and Dad that I was leaving and Mom said, "Bryan, aren't you going to eat anything?" I said, "No thanks Mom, I'm not hungry."

It was a very nice June evening and Johnny propped the Legion doors open with folding chairs. The Legion had an outstanding dance floor and stage. We carried our equipment in and set things up. Johnny said, "OK boys, listen up. I'm looking for a large crowd tonight and I want you to give them a good show!" Some kids were already gathering on the steps and landing in front of the building. "Now let's see what you sound like!" Johnny continued. We doubled checked our tuning as Steve adjusted his high-hat cymbal. I looked at the guys and started our signature song, *Bull Dog*. We had just gotten into it when

Johnny raised his hands and yelled, "Stop!" When the room silenced he said, "Guys, turn it up a little more, this place will be packed." Gaiter, Doug, and I turned to our Fender piggy-back amps and increased the master volume. When we turned around Johnny was standing at the doorway and said with excitement, "Give it to me again!" I started the song off as usual and everyone fell in. Johnny clapped his hands to our music and smiled. We finished the song and Steve wanted to do a vocal so we did a portion of *Twist and Shout*. Johnny gave his approval and said, "Boys, let's go downstairs and take a break," as he held his arms wide to herd us towards the stairs.

We could hear the kids overhead as we nervously waited in the basement. By the commotion, there was a large crowd already and we still had thirty minutes before we were to start. Johnny went upstairs to collect the admission fee and watch the stage after he gave us all a 'that-a-boy.' He had two rubber stamps specially made that said "The Silhouettes" and he and two girls, Peggy and Donna were busy at the door taking the money and stamping hands.

Johnny came downstairs and gave us our final pep-talk. Again he opened his arms and herded us towards the stairway leading to the stage. We had placed our blue flood lights on the front edge of the stage. They were not turned on as we put our guitar straps over our shoulders and Steve made a last minute adjustment to his stool. Johnny was just off stage with the plug for the blue flood lights in his hand hovering over an extension cord socket lying at his feet. He smiled and giving a thumbs-up, plugged in the lights and said, "Give it to them Boys!" We were drenched in blue light and wild screams erupted as I started *Bull Dog*. When Steve rolled off on the drums the dance floor was filled with girls, out numbering the guys four to one, dancing, screaming, and waving their arms. Johnny made his way back to the double entry doors before the song was over and he seemed just as excited as the fans. Every time one of us made eye contact with him, he gave a smile and his traditional thumbs up. We all realized how important Johnny was to us that night. His skills in promotion were excellent and we relied more and more on his adult guidance.

The Silhouettes performed again at the Legion and at the Fair that July with the proceeds paying for an extension of the pavilion off the Arts Hall.

Chapter 12
The Trip

The first week of football practice was always tough. We practiced two times a day the two weeks before school began. By the end of the second week we were somewhat in shape and worked on fundamentals more than running and conditioning. Tom and Gaiter helped in the locker room and carried the title of equipment managers. They collected the dirty uniforms and washed them for the team. They sat in a small room with a dutch door. The room was about five feet wide and eight feet deep. In the room they had cardboard drums to collect the dirty clothes. The jerseys in one, the pants in another and tee-shirts and jock straps in another cardboard drum with rolls of white tape and ace bandages on small shelves. The team took pleasure in making life tough for Tom and Gaiter. After practice we would throw our sweaty tee-shirts and jocks at them rather than in the cardboard drums. On the second Friday we finished practice running seven laps around the outside perimeter of the gridiron and when we entered the locker room there was a message on the chalk board that read, "I quit, Tom and Gaiter." The team took no mercy in making life miserable for them that day.

It turned out that the joke was on us. The third week we practiced without clean uniforms. Thankfully the coach replaced Tom and Gaiter at the end of that miserable week.

The Junior Class was divided in half alphabetically for driver's training. Half of the students would take the class this autumn and the second half this spring. I was in the first half. The driver's training teacher was Mr. Burns. All the guys looked forward to driver's training but the girls had mixed feelings about the class.

The first three weeks were spent in the classroom and we would be administered the state written test. Upon passing we were issued our driving permits which allowed us to drive with a licensed driver twenty-one years old or older. Many of us guys had experience behind the wheel. I had driven my Dodge up and down the alley and out in the country many times. The guys who lived on the farm had been driving grain trucks from the time they could reach the pedals, and see over the dash. Friday in driver's training class, Mr. Burns asked Charles, Bob, and I if we could log some hours Saturday in the driver's training car. He said to tell our parents that we would be busy driving most of the morning and afternoon. He said to meet him at the high school at nine o'clock Saturday or be sure to contact him that evening at the football game if for some reason we could not make it.

Most other schools were larger than us and tonight wasn't any different. We were in the locker room and dressed. The coach said, "Guys, let's have a good warm up." We exited the locker room and climbed the small ridge to field level to the overwhelming chant, "Beat, beat, beat, the blue!" Our opponents were lined up eight abreast from the goal line to the forty yard line. Sociologically they had just won the game unless some strange fate intervened. We were dwarfed by the opposing team. They were big and there were a lot of them. We lined up across the opposing forty yard line and started doing jumping jacks chanting, "Beat, beat, beat, the Tigers!" I don't think any one could hear us over their chants. We ran through a few plays and returned to the locker room. The coach was fired up. He said, "You can beat those guys! Make the first hit count! Let them know who is boss!" I'm sure many of us were thinking, they have already done that. We huddled up and clasped our hands thrusting them down and back up three times and on the fourth time we all said "break," thus separating and leaving the locker room for the second time. We were welcomed onto the field by our loyal fans, cheerleaders and the marching band playing *On Wisconsin*. We all made our way to the sideline and the captain and co-captain, Terry and Tank walked to center field and met with the officials and opposing team captains for the coin flip. The official indicated we won the flip and asked Terry if we wanted to receive or kick. Terry chose to receive which the official signaled. He instructed captains and co-captains to shake hands and wished all a good game. Terry and Tank jogged back to the side line where we were huddled for the second time around Coach. We joined hands again as he reminded us to make that first hit count.

By the end of the first quarter the visitors had made substitutions of their second and third string players. We were behind twenty-one to zero. By the half, the score was thirty-five to zero. We managed to score a touchdown the second half but failed on the extra point making the final score thirty-five to six. We were glad to see the game come to a close.

We showered and some of us made the walk uptown to the Highway. All the stools at the counter were occupied when we got there so Tank and I decided to walk down to Murph's. There we met Bob who was standing outside with one foot resting about a foot up on the wall as he leaned on the window ledge. I ask Bob if he was looking forward to driving tomorrow and he said he was but not overly excited. Les joined our line up against the store front. Les and I talked about a Go-Kart we had built. It had been several weeks since we rode it. I told Les it needed some work. We both were excited about the prospect of having our driver's license and the Go-Kart soon would be history. We talked about cars, girls, and our losing football season until Tank said, "Boys, I'm going home." We all decided that was a good idea so we walked our separate directions home.

Hoss on the field

Saturday morning I left home and walked down the alley towards the high school. I got there five minutes before nine o'clock. Charles and Bob were already standing by the drivers training car but Mr. Burns wasn't there yet. We hung around until about ten after and our teacher arrived. He got out of his old station wagon and unlocked the driver's education car. "Who wants to drive first?" Mr. Burns ask. Charles said, "I will, if no one else wants to." Mr. Burns nodded and went back to his car and picked up a copy of the morning newspaper. Bob and I got into the back seat as Charles got behind the wheel with Mr. Burns riding shot gun. Charles ask, "Where to?" Mr. Burns said, "Guys, lets go to Indy." Bob and I looked at one another with surprise. Bob then lipped, Indy with an exaggerated look of surprise on his face. I shrugged my shoulders and Charles said, "Indy?" Mr. Burns said, "Yah, we might as well go some place instead of wasting time and money driving in circles around town." Charles put the car in first gear and towards Indianapolis we went. Mr. Burns opened the newspaper to the sports section and seemed to be amused about the story of our loss last night, paying no attention to Charles and the busiest strip of highway in the mid-west. After an hour and a half, Mr. Burns instructed Charles to pull over the next chance he had at a filling station. Soon Charles pulled off US 40 and into a Sinclair Station. We all took turns using the restroom, after Mr. Burns. He smoked a cigarette while Bob and I drank Cokes. Charles stood on the walk that ran beside the building leading to the restrooms, not joining us. Mr. Burns finished his smoke and said as he twisted his brown shoe grinding the butt into the concrete, "Bob it's your turn." Bob opened the car door and adjusted the seat. As we continued east on US 40 Charles didn't say anything. I figured he wanted to continue to drive and was angry about Mr. Burns asking Bob. I figured that's what we were there for, to get our hours logged.

As we approached Indy, Mr. Burns gave instructions to Bob as he drove through the Saturday morning traffic. "Turn right at the next stop light then go four blocks and turn left," Mr. Burns said. Bob made the right turn and Mr. Burns looked back at Charles and me saying, "We'll go to the race track." He continued giving Bob directions and by eleven thirty we were setting at the Indianapolis Motor Speedway. "If you have a couple bucks to burn the Speedway Museum is open," Mr. Burns said. Bob and I walked over to the museum and decided to check it out. We both enjoyed the old roadsters on display. Mr. Burns finished his paper while sitting on a bench in front of the museum. We didn't see Charles until we exited the museum. I asked Bob, "I wonder what's wrong with Charles?" Bob said, "I wouldn't worry about him, he just wanted to drive longer."

Bob and I joined Mr. Burns on the bench and Charles appeared in the distance walking towards the car. Mr. Burns said, "Well I guess it's time to head back. Why is Charles acting like he is?" Bob said, "Well, he's always been a strange duck." Mr. Burns said, "Your right, Bob! He is a strange one, for sure." As we made our way towards the car I noticed Mr. Burns' newspaper on the bench. The light breeze had turned a few pages of the paper and it appeared the paper would soon be carried across the parking lot. I ask, "Mr. Burns, do you want your paper?" He answered, "Nope, I'm done with it." As we reached the car he told Bob to drive again and turned towards me and said, "We'll let Bob get his time in then you can drive the rest of the way home." Charles rolled his eyes and I looked around to see pages of the newspaper blowing across the parking lot.

Bob drove for about thirty minutes and Mr. Burns instructed him to pull off the highway the next chance he had. Soon we were going through a town and they had a McDonalds. Bob pulled into the restaurant and we all got cheeseburgers and fries with a large Coke except Charles who got a fish sandwich. We ate and I traded places with Bob and drove west, crossing the Illinois State line and continued toward home on US 40.

The Silhouettes were booked to play a sock hop at our rival town Casey, six miles west. I was especially anxious to play there because of a girl named Barbara whom I knew from the past. She was a cheerleader and I wanted to ask her for a date.

The guys were at the barn earlier than normal that Saturday evening, although Johnny had not showed up with the U-Haul yet. I think we all were looking forward to playing tonight. We had added a new member to the group. Kirk would play the organ. Many new songs had an organ track and Kirk played well. Johnny pulled into the drive and into the back yard so he could back the U-Haul close to the door of the practice room in the barn. It took him several times jockeying the trailer back and forth to get orientated correctly with the U-Haul close to the door and the car pointed toward the street. Johnny had a camera and said, "Boys, I need to take some pictures of you." I went into the practice room and got my guitar and rejoined the guys as Johnny led us behind the barn to a large limb that was downed by a spring storm. He posed us around and on the limb and took several pictures and just as fast said, "Let's get her loaded Boys!" We developed a certain way of stacking the equipment in the U-Haul and it didn't take long to get everything aboard.

On the way I told the guys about driving to Indy and going through the Museum. Doug was the only band member old enough to take driver's training and he was scheduled for the second class. Gaiter and Kirk had one year to wait before they could get their permit.

Last summer Gaiter had gotten in trouble for driving his mom's car to the ball park. I remembered the day his mom purchased a beautiful wine red Pontiac Bonneville two door with a black vinyl top. The car was new and she had just brought it home. Billy, Gaiter and I had returned to town after spending the afternoon swimming at the lake. We were watching Gaiter pour water on some carbide he dumped on the sidewalk from a blue can. It started to bubble and he then lit a match and held it next to the bubbling gray pieces of carbide which now were emitting white foam and a hazy vapor. Like magic, the vapor started to flame, Billy and I watched in amazement. Neither Billy nor I had seen carbide before. We decided to come back after supper to see what it looked like after dark.

After supper I met Billy in his front yard and we crossed the road on our bicycles making crow calls, as we approached the front of Gaiter's house. We heard a faint 'back here' and ran around the side of the house towards the back yard. Gaiter showed us a large fire cracker which he called an M-80. Billy said, "Set it off Gaiter!" Gaiter said he wanted to wait until it was good and dark.

I walked over to the new wine red Bonneville and looked inside. The car was the most beautiful car I had ever seen. I was admiring the black leather seats when I noticed the keys in the ignition. I turned towards Billy and Gaiter and said, "Gaiter, your Mom left the keys in the car! You should take it for a test drive." Gaiter just sat on the grass messing around with a short piece of pipe and didn't respond to what I just said. I walked towards Gaiter and Billy. Billy said to Gaiter, "Hey, take it for a spin!" Gaiter looked at Billy and shook his head from side to side and returned his attention to the pipe. I asked him, "What is the pipe for?" Gaiter said, "I think I'll make a cannon with it." One end was threaded and the other end wasn't. "All I need is a cap with a hole drilled in it." Billy changed the conversation by saying, "I dare you to take your Mom's car for a drive." Gaiter again did not say anything but he got up and slowly walked towards the new car. He opened the driver's door and sat behind the wheel. Billy and I looked at one another in amazement because we never thought that he would actually drive the car. Gaiter adjusted the power seat all the way forward and up but still could barley see over the dash board. Then Billy and I heard the car start! Then the car started backing down the drive. Billy and I ran to the front of Gaiter's house and watched him back the beautiful large Pontiac onto the street. From the look on Billy's face I think he felt like he should not have dared Gaiter. I was just as surprised, and wished I hadn't suggested driving the car to him. Gaiter took off rather fast but did not squeal the tires. Billy and I were both so shocked by what was happening that we just stood there staring blankly at the street where the car was. Gaiter turned east and was out of sight before either of us spoke. Finally I said, "I wonder where he is going?" Billy said, "I don't know, but I hope he heads back soon!" Billy had an extra incentive to see Gaiter return. Billy's dad was an Illinois State Trooper! If Gaiter got caught driving and said anything about us daring him Billy would get it! We walked across the street and sat on Billy's porch waiting for the big red car to return.

After about fifteen minutes, which seemed like an hour, the Bonneville returned with a state squad car following close behind! Billy's younger brother, Angel was playing little league baseball and Billy's dad had been at the park watching the young players when a car entered the outfield, and left as quickly. The game was temporarily halted and the coaches waved in their players as a safety precaution. Billy's dad pursued Gaiter in the state squad car with the red lights on! Billy's dad did not realize at the time that it was Gaiter nor did he recognize the brand new Pontiac Bonneville.

Gaiter pulled the car into his driveway with Billy's dad close behind. When Gaiter stopped, Billy's dad quickly approached the driver's door, opened it, and grabbed Gaiter by the arm and jerked him from the car. He grabbed the other free arm and started yelling while he shook Gaiter to the rhythm of his voice! The conversation finished with Billy's dad saying something to the effect that if that happened again Gaiter would find himself in reform school.

Billy's dad returned to the ball park and Gaiter returned to the small whitish-gray piles of spent carbide and the pipe. After Billy and I were sure the coast was clear we rejoined Gaiter. Billy asked Gaiter, "What did Dad say?" Gaiter just smiled and said, "Very little." He then stood and removed the M-80 from his shirt pocket placing it into the end of the clothesline post. He returned to the car and took a Kool cigarette from a pack his mom had left on the passenger seat. He slowly returned to the clothesline post with the unlit cigarette held between his lips. He removed a book of matches from his jean pocket and lit the cigarette and took a deep drag as he replaced the book of matches in his pocket. He casually looked up at the M-80 and took the lit cigarette touching the black fuse. A small spark, then white smoke exited the horizontal pipe of the clothesline pole as Billy and I ran towards the barn. Gaiter calmly walked a few feet away and squatted down placing his fingers in his ears. The boom rocked the neighborhood! Gaiter calmly returned to the short pipe lying on the ground, sitting down and twisting the pipe in his hands while in deep thought. Billy said, "I'm going home before he explodes another fire cracker." I thought that would be a good idea too but I didn't want to go inside right away. I hoped that Mom and Dad would think I was in the back yard when the M-80 rattled the windows! Mom must of saw me crossing the street and stuck her head out the screen door and said, "What was that explosion?" "Gaiter touched off an M-80," I said. I could tell Mom wasn't happy; I should have answered her differently. I didn't know if she knew what an M-80 was. I didn't until Gaiter produced one.

Our thoughts shifted from M-80's to learning new songs and performing as the weeks past. But the Bonneville, it was a cool car!

We arrived at the Casey High School and started moving our equipment into the old gym. We all were excited about playing there. First, we expected a large turn out; secondly it was almost as fun as playing at home. It would be largely the same crowd. We quickly sat up and began tuning our guitars. Johnny walked to the opposite side of the gym and said, "Ok boys, let's hear it!" We played *Bull Dog* about half way through and Johnny stopped us and asked to hear *96 Tears*. I counted, one, two, three, four and Kirk played the intro and we all fell in. Steve started the vocal, Johnny held up his hands and we stopped. "Give me a little more volume on the vocals," he said. I turned up the PA and counted off again. It wasn't long until Johnny gave us his approval by a thumbs up. We left the gymnasium and entered a hallway above the bleachers. We could see the gym floor through a door that opened to the bleachers. We watched the people come into the gym. It was rather warm and it was going to get hot in the old gym by the end of the evening. The only air circulation came from doors at each end of the gym that opened into hallways.

At five to eight Johnny gave us our usual pep talk. "Boys, I want it tight tonight! Let's get down there and give it to them!" We walked the hallways leading to the set of doors on the east end of the gym. The gym was crowded with Casey and Martinsville kids and some from other towns too. We played trying to be heard above the screams and cheers. Actually all the noise made it much easer to play. We knew they couldn't hear any small mistakes.

After the first four songs I saw Barbara and two other girls making their way towards us. I turned and told the guys, "Let's play *Barbara Ann*." I started the vocal choirs and I was self conscious about starting the song without any music. The other guys had to follow me and then the music came in. I always imagined that I would start off key and the song would need to be restarted. I would play F sharp; the key the song started in and turn away from the mic singing "Barb, Barb, Barb" quietly and when I felt comfortable turn back to the mic and start the song. It worked out well. Barbara and her friends were standing in front of us just as I started the song. I knew she was impressed!

We took our break returning to the hallway above the gym and bleachers. Kirk didn't join us and I asked Doug where he was. Doug said, "Ah, he is talking to some tall blond." I looked out the door down on the gym floor and saw him talking to a girl wearing white with blond hair. The distance was such that I couldn't see them well so I decided to go back down to the gym floor and take a closer look. I approached Kirk and the girl and Kirk smiled and said, "Debby I would like for you to meet Bryan." Her long blond hair was parted on the side and covered her eyes. Debby slightly moved her hair as to recognize me and smiled. I said, "Glad to meet you Debby." As Kirk and I returned to where we were set up on the gym floor I told him, "Kirk, if you don't ask Debby out I'd like too." He said, "Hoss I'll say something to her if you would like." I smiled and said, "Thanks!"

Monday we were talking about a rumor circulating around school about Mr. Burns. Apparently he mentioned something to someone that the school board requested him to be present at the board meeting Thursday night. I was wondering if it was concerning our trip to Indy. Tank said he figured it was about something he said in Science class. He was a good guy, anyway us guys thought so, and we sure didn't want to see him in trouble, even though he was a teacher.

All week we had wondered about the rumor concerning Mr. Burns and the school board meeting and tonight was the meeting. Tank suggested that the football team go to the meeting in support of him. It was a good idea but we all knew our parents would not allow us to attend. We got the scoop early Friday morning. It seems that Mr. Burns was questioned about a comment he made in Science class and also instructed not to take the driver's training car no more than ten miles from the high school. The guys were unhappy about the board calling him to the meeting but happy that he got by with just a hand slap. We also concluded that Charles said something about driving to Indy to his parents and they contacted the superintendent or a school board member. This we never would know for sure.

Chapter 13
The Egg

Newsweek and *US News and World Report* escalated their reports on Vietnam as the warm weather of summer gave way to autumn. Young people became more and more involved protesting the war. We had a geographical advantage in the heart of the Midwest or possibility a disadvantage, depending on how it was perceived. Even though we were experiencing world events nightly on television, the atrocity of war in a distant place seemed a long way away for us. We began to take note because kids our age were protesting in cities across the country especially on the west coast.

After lunch we went to study hall and many of us were wishing we were outside on this unusually nice autumn day. I was hoping to get in another day swimming at the lake Saturday afternoon. I had said something to Gaiter but didn't get a response. The band was playing at the Loft in Terre Haute Saturday evening and Gaiter had been working on two new Rolling Stone songs. We were rehearsing tonight and Thursday night. I expected him to introduce the songs tonight. If everything went well I planned on bringing up going swimming Saturday after practice.

Study hall ended with a laugh as Larry approached the study hall monitor's desk. He took a text book to Mr. Medsker and with a very serious expression, asked him a question about the American Revolution. Mr. Medsker was enthused to help Larry with American History. First, it was very unusual for a student to approach a study hall teacher for help of any kind and secondly, Mr. Medsker taught history. Larry succeeded in hoodwinking him. The underlying purpose of Larry's inquiry was to visually act like a mix between a chimpanzee and a contortionist without Mr. Medsker noticing. Laughter rose as the teacher immersed himself in the American Revolution while Larry skillfully looked absurd. The bell rang. Larry quickly removed his history book from the grasp of Mr. Medsker and joined the laughing students crowding through the study hall doors into the hallway leaving our unsuspecting history teacher bewildered in his abrupt departure.

A group of guys which consisted mainly of our next hour Industrial Arts Class were huddling behind the bleachers. They were collectively holding and admiring a torn out centerfold from a girly magazine. I wedged my way into the pack to take a look but it was short lived. It was about time for the second bell. The guys broke up and hustled to their classes. Some of us left the old building and entered the new building walking through the empty cafeteria. The tables were folded up against the walls, and placed there after lunch each day. The Industrial Arts Classroom was on the east side of the building and next door was the Superintendents' office.

Tank, Hoss, Charles, and Bob

As we walked by the classroom the Captain, our nickname for the Industrial Arts teacher, was talking to the coach at the double doors that opened into the new gymnasium. Several guys already had entered the classroom before me and a few others. Upon entering the room there was an unexplained excitement. Bob pointed towards the blackboard which was actually green, behind the small podium that was used by the Captain. Someone had attached the centerfold to the blackboard. The last bell rang and we took our places and as the Captain entered the classroom and stepped behind the small podium that sat on a desk, "Good afternoon," he said. "Today we will devote our lecture time to 'proper gluing techniques'." We pretended to pay attention as he started, but in reality, the picture behind the Captain was our focus. The Captain was enjoying the lecture as much as we appeared to be because for once he thought we were giving him our full attention. The lecture concluded with the Captain saying, "Boys I really want to thank you for your attention today." He shuffled a few pages of notes and stepped to his right to place them on his desk and his eye caught something but he dismissed it. As he was laying the papers on his desk he took a second look at the blackboard and we knew that he realized the picture was there, and in fact, it was the object of our attention. He removed the picture from the board and carefully pulled the scotch tape from the corners, folded the picture at its center crease and looking up, spread a gaze of disapproval across the room making eye contact with each one of us. It was difficult to hold back the urge to laugh as he glared at us in disgust. Bob seemed to have an extra sense of fulfillment in the Captain's apparent disappointment, remembering his hours spent under a work bench baaing like a lamb. Exactly at the correct moment, the Captain spoke saying, "I knew it was too good to be true," and the class erupted in laughter. He took the folded picture and held it over the large trash can beside his desk and with a smile let it drop into the container.

All of us but Doug were at the Barn at six thirty including Johnny. Johnny said, "I need to find something to build a fire under Doug." Gaiter and I tuned our guitars as Steve adjusted his drum equipment. Doug came in and Johnny said, "Glad you could make it Doug." He got his bass out of the case and turned on his amp. As the amps were warming up Johnny said that Gaiter had two new songs and wanted us to work on them for Saturday at the Loft.

After practice Kirk said he told Debby that I would like to have a date with her. I replied, "What did she say?" He said, "She asked me if you had your driver's license. I told her no but you would this summer." "Did she say anything else?" I asked. "Yah, she said she would like to get to know you better."

Doug said he had a larger gas heater that we could use

this winter and Johnny said, "Good, let's get it installed." Doug said something about buying stove pipe and Johnny told him get what ever we need and we'll take the money out of the kitty to reimburse you. "Can you install it?" Johnny asked him, Doug nodded and said, "Yes". Johnny again said, "Let's get it done!"

Before the first bell Wednesday morning Huck and I were standing against the gym wall close to the bleachers. He said that he wanted to show me something and I said, "What?" Huck replied, "Follow me," and we went behind the bleachers to his locker. He carefully worked the combination and removed the lock bail from the handle of the locker. He looked both directions down the poorly lit hallway for the possible curiosity seeker. After he was certain the coast was clear, he removed a small brown sack from his coat pocket hanging in the locker. I said, "What's that?" Huck carefully peeled the paper sack open exposing a brown chicken egg. I was disappointed. I was hoping on something like a snake or frog, but an egg? Then Huck stated to explain his plan. First he told me the egg was rotten and what he wanted to do with it. To my delight, Huck suggested putting the egg inside of Mr. Medsker's hat. He giggled as he painted the picture of Mr. Medsker removing his hat from the nail above the black board and the rotten egg falling to the floor busting. Huck ask, "Think it will work?" I said, "Sure!" Huck said, "I'll need you to watch for him and I will sneak into the room between classes and put the egg under the hat. All we need to do is get it under the hat before seventh hour." Seventh hour was our History class and the last class of the day. We knew that after class and as we were leaving Mr. Medsker would remove his gray Fedora from the nail because he left as soon as class dismissed unless a student had a question which was a rarity. No one would stay after school to discuss class work unless it was a teachers pet.

Mr. Medsker was Study Hall Monitor again today and Huck and I thought we may have a chance to get the egg placed after Study Hall, between classes. Huck said we needed someone or something to distract Mr. Medsker just as the Study Hall dismissal bell rang. I said, "What about Larry?" Huck said, "See if you can get him to go up to the desk right before the bell rings." I said, "I'll get that set up." Huck continued, "Larry can pretend to ask him another question. You can stand in the hall in front of the History class door and be my look-out, I'll put the egg under his hat while Larry distracts Medsker." I gave Huck a smile of approval. I quietly walked across the Study Hall towards the Library and signaled Larry to join me. The wall between the Library and Study Hall had large glass windows about four feet up from the floor that ran the length of the wall. The rule was, only two Study Hall students could be in the Library at once. The windows provided a way for the Study Hall Monitor to observe activities in the Library because the librarian was sometimes busy elsewhere. I was watching discreetly between the books neatly stacked on the shelf as Larry made his way towards the Library. I told him about Huck's plan and he agreed to distract Mr. Medsker just before the dismissal bell. I made my way back where I was sitting in the Study Hall, followed soon after by Larry. I gave Huck a smile and nod of confidence, signifying Larry was with us.

About two minutes prior to the dismissal bell, Larry approached the Study Hall Monitor's desk with his History text book. He waited for Mr. Medsker to acknowledge him and laid the open book on the desk. He began the plan of deception just as the bell rang. Huck and I quickly left the study hall and crossed the hallway. Huck entered the empty History classroom and I took my position by the doorway. It didn't take long for Huck to place the rotten egg under the Fedora hanging on its nail over the black board. We departed the area without being noticed. As we walked down the stairs we snickered about what might happen. When we entered the Captain's room in the new building we talked about the prank with Larry. The possibilities of what was to come entertained us through most of Industrial Arts Class.

We hurriedly exchanged books to the sound of metal locker doors slamming closed behind the bleachers and made our way towards History Class. Everybody in Industrial Arts Class knew of the egg except Charles. James, usually quiet, took a special delight in the idea. I looked towards him as I took my seat and he smiled and he gave me an OK sign. The class dragged on and on. Mr. Medsker loved history, and would become so wrapped up in the event he was explaining to his students that he sometimes would become impervious to his current surroundings. This seemed to be the case today. Tank broke the monotony of the lecture by coughing and discreetly inserting the word egg at the end of the cough. Tank did a good job, as always, turning a lackluster class into a comical treat.

Our anticipation was at a new height when the bell finally rang. As planned, Huck, Bob, and I stopped in front of the classroom door, in the hallway, and started a bogus conversation waiting for Mr. Medsker to remove his hat from the nail over the chalk board. We were joined by Tank and James. We watched Mr. Medsker clear his desk and carefully place his materials inside the desk drawers. He pushed his wooden office chair under the desk and walked to the end of the blackboard next to the doorway. He reached up and grasped the Fedora by the creased point on the top-front of the expensive hat and lifted it off the nail. The rotten egg fell down and hit the chalk tray, exploding with the majority of the rotten, slimly stench splattering on his crotch! On a scale of one to ten, this was a ten! We quickly scattered like surprised cockroaches and regrouped to the relative safety of the dark corridor behind the bleachers. We exchanged pats on the back, stored our books, slammed the locker doors shut, and placed the bail of the combination lock through the handle locking the lock. We continued to laugh about Mr. Medsker's demise as we parted going our separate ways toward home.

I met Gaiter in the student parking lot and told him about the prank we pulled on Mr. Medsker. I ask Gaiter again about going swimming Saturday suggesting that it may be our last chance of the season. He gave a nod of approval.

The weather was great Saturday, not too windy and unseasonably warm. Right after lunch I went to Gaiters. He was running a model airplane engine. Gaiter had mounted the engine on a board and nailed the board on his front porch. The engine had a propeller on it and was loud. I watched as Gaiter ran the engine waiting for him to shut it off or for it to run out of fuel. Finally, the engine stopped. Gaiter said, "What do you think about this Forster?" I said, "It's the biggest I have ever seen." Gaiter smiled proudly and said, "It's a Forster 99!" I looked it over and asked him where he got it and he said from Johnny.

"Well, are you ready to go swimming?" I asked. Gaiter said, "Yah, wait for me to get this engine off the porch." I knew he really was proud of the Forster model airplane engine because usually he would leave airplane engines, old Maytag washer engines, or whatever mounted on the outer edge of the front porch until the space was needed for something else or the engine was beyond repair and pitched behind the barn.

Gaiter carefully removed the engine and took it into the house. I waited on the porch. After a few minutes he came out and we rode our bikes towards the lake. I passed my drivers test in July although it took two attempts. It was said that four out of five boys failed the driver's test the first time. Girls had to do something really bad to fail. I guess the state license examiners wanted us boys to be more appreciative of our new privilege. My old Dodge was beyond driving on the road. This summer I decided I would convert it into a convertible and actually cut the top off. Because it was a four door, removing the top was a bad idea. I was test driving it soon after the surgery; in the middle of a corner the right side bowed out and the doors swung open. The rear doors were hinged at the rear and opened opposite from the front doors. This put so much stress on the remaining body that the rear door and fender ended almost horizontal. I made a hasty repair by installing a length of pipe behind the front seat and securing the middle side posts to the ends but this didn't last long. Eventually I removed everything from the dashboard back. The Captain said he would take the car and make it a teaching aid and fortunately for him and unfortunately for me, the old Dodge was soon to have another home, within the confines of the Industrial Arts Shop.

We rode down Mule Hill and Gaiter, as usual, beat me to the bridge. We crossed and stopped at the highway and waited our opportunity to cross. Soon we were crossing the dam at the lake. There already were eight or more kids there. Gaiter and I walked down to the boat house and said hi to TC, John, and Janice. Mike had driven his new Bridgestone motorcycle which was parked beside John's car. Mike was out on the raft getting ready to jump off the springboard. There were a few others in the water and on the raft. Gaiter and I pulled our tee-shirts over our heads and took turns diving from the dock into the warm water. We swam out to the raft and Gaiter climbed the ladder to the high board and made a beautiful dive slicing the water upon entry like a knife. I jumped off the spring board doing a cannon ball. While swimming back to the ladder on the side of the raft I said hi to Mike and told him his Bridgestone looked nice. To my surprise Mike said, "Hoss, you want to take her for a spin?" I was so surprised and hurried to answer I gulped some water down the wrong pipe and when I finished coughing I answered, "Sure, that would be great!" Another car crossed the dam and parked by the others. We saw three girls walking down to the boat house but because of the distance and glare from the water, I couldn't tell who they were. Gaiter climbed back up to the high diving board and made another beautiful jackknife dive. Gaiter and Johnny both were excellent divers. Mike said, as we treaded water, "The key is in it, go ahead and take it for a spin when you want to." I thanked him and climbed up the ladder and made a dive from the spring board. I didn't want to appear too anxious but, I wanted to swim back to the dock immediately.

I stood on the dock for a few minutes, allowing the water to drip from my trunks and the sun dry my wet back. I didn't see the girls who had just walked down from the parked cars. They must be in the boat house changing clothes. After a few more minutes I walked up to the motorcycle. After looking it over, I swung my right leg over the black imitation leather seat. I wasn't experienced when it came to motorcycles. I had only driven one once before and it wasn't actually a motorcycle but a Honda Moped. I shifted the gear shift with my left toes to feel the shifting pattern and remembered Mike saying, first down, neutral, second, third, and fourth was the pattern. I pulled the clutch lever and positioned the lever in neutral, turned the key on and swiveled the peg out on the kick starter. The Bridgestone came to life after the second kick. I toed the shifter down and the motorcycle made a clicking sound. I twisted the throttle and slowly let out the clutch lever and drove through the parking area. I drove across the dam and towards the house which was about a half mile away. I turned around at the shed along the road just before reaching the house. This is where the grounds keeper stored the mowing equipment and the road was wide enough to turn around. Heading back I crossed the dam and saw someone standing by the parked cars. I didn't recognize who it was until I was stopped and she smiled and approached me. It was Donna. She was one of the three girls who just arrived a few minutes ago. "Hi Donna," I said. She said, "Hello Bryan. Is that your motorcycle?" I told her no, it was Mike's. I had never seen Donna with her hair down. She always wore it in a tight bun at school. I was taken by the length of her blond hair which almost reached her waist. "Will you take me for a ride?" Donna asked. I said, "Climb on." She sat on the seat behind me and I retraced my previous path across the dam, to the storage shed and back. When we returned to the parking area she thanked me and we walked down to the dock. I dove into the water which felt cool after being in the bright sun for some time.

I reminded Gaiter that we need to leave by three-thirty so we could get ready for our trip to Terre Haute. Johnny said he wanted to leave by five our time. Terre Haute was an hour ahead of us. Gaiter made his last high dive of the season and we asked the guys at the dock if anyone was going to the Loft tonight. Lynn said she was but I doubted it. The Loft was on the second floor of a Wabash Avenue store in downtown Terre Haute. It was always over crowded, and the kids were not overly friendly but it gave us great exposure. Johnny was always thinking ahead.

We played to a jam packed dance floor. It was hot on the second floor, and we were happy when it was time for us to do the last song. We had to carry all the equipment down the flight of stairs to load the U-Haul. Actually, it was much more than a flight. We arrived home about midnight and after unloading the U-Haul we all went home instead of making the rounds uptown.

Sunday we awoke to a brisk sunny day. There was a feeling in the air that summer was over. I briefly went out but it was cool enough that I decided to go back in. I went into the living room and took my usual position lying on the floor in front of the television. The Sunday news show was on. Dad always watched the Sunday morning talk shows. They were reporting about the first major ground operation in Vietnam. According to the reporter, 1500 Viet Cong made an attack on the American airfield at Chu Lai. The reporter said 45 Marines were killed and 120 were wounded. The Viet Cong suffered 614 dead and 9 taken prisoner. The Army officer who was being interviewed said, "This first victory gives a big boost to US Troop morale."

Chapter 14
In and Out

Returning to school after Christmas vacation is always a drag. Our study hall after lunch had been replaced with a mandatory Health Class. It was held twice a week on Tuesdays and Thursdays for eight weeks. The class was held in the building behind the high school teachers' parking area. The two story building's first floor contained the janitor's supplies, mowing equipment, and the washer and dryer used by the athletic managers. The second floor was used as a classroom for Driver's Training and Health Class.

We walked across the teachers' parking area towards the stairs leading up the north side of the building. The classroom was unusually warm unlike the teacher who was all business. Few of us liked Mr. Stikes. He was a peculiar small man that seldom if ever smiled. He handed out a thirty page booklet that he said was ours to keep. It had short paragraphs about such things as head lice to athlete's foot. It wasn't proper to discuss sexually transmitted diseases in a mixed class but most of us guys found that small section in the back of the book as soon as possible.

Mr. Stikes returned to the podium and asked us to open the book and we would read the first two pages prior to a class discussion about skin conditions. Huck, Bob, Tank, James, TC, and I were sitting in the back row and Tank started his coughing routine. It wasn't long until Mr. Stikes became agitated with Tank and told him to either control his cough or leave the classroom. This brought a round of laughter, which in turn, aggravated the teacher more.

Huck was doing the old hand under the armpit noise although he had developed it to a state of perfection. He could make the noise by contorting his shoulder without placing his hand under his arm! As the class progressed Huck strategically included his noisy eruptions at the end of Mr. Stikes comments. Mr. Stikes became angrier and many of us were on the verge of breaking into a hysterical laugh. Huck masterfully made another and it was more than I could take. I started to laugh uncontrollably soon to be joined by many other classmates. Mr. Stikes was furious. He glared at me as I wiped the tears of laughter from my eyes and said, "You may leave the class! Leave now and don't come back!" I walked out of the room into the cool air and made my way across the teacher's parking lot into the old building and downstairs to the boy's restroom where I spent the rest of the period.

Early the next morning I looked up Mr. Stikes, apologized for laughing, and told him I wasn't making the noise. He frowned at me and said, "My decision stands." The next best course of action I thought was to ask to meet with the principal and tell him my side of the story hoping he would intervene. The next day I entered the principal's office and ask the student office aid if I could speak to the Principal. She stepped into the doorway opening into his office and asked him if he had a moment to speak to a student. I heard him say yes and she turned and motioned me to step around the counter and into the inner office. Nervously, I walked into his office. Mr. Tucker said, "Good morning Bryan. How may I help you?" I told him that I had been instructed to leave health class and Mr. Stikes would not let me return. I went on to say that I laughed but wasn't making the noise. I also explained that I approached Mr. Stikes and apologized but he said his decision was final. Mr. Tucker said, "Bryan, are you asking me to intercede?" I said, "Yes, would you please speak to him?" Mr. Tucker said he would, but he would stand behind his final decision. Later that day Mr. Tucker approached me in the hallway and told me that Mr. Stikes was maintaining his position and his decision would be upheld. Mr. Tucker also said that Health Class was a pre-requisite for graduation so I would need to take the class next year. I caught myself before I said crap, but that word rushed through my mind like a bolt of lighting as I stood looking at the unsympathetic face of the principal. I caught my wits and thanked him for speaking to Mr. Stikes on my behalf.

Friday morning everyone was talking about TC. The story was the topic of discussion. TC accidently shot himself! No one knew how serious. The news had put a damper on the last day of the week. Everyone respected TC and we were all very concerned. It was the main topic after lunch. In fact, the girls were not playing the record player and dancing in the old gym but standing around in small groups talking about the fate of TC. The first bell rang and Huck, Bob, and I joined James on the way to class in the new building. We all were distraught about TC as our imaginations ran rampant through the morning and our emotions were especially raw when we entered the classroom and noticed his empty desk and chair, as obvious as a neon sign.

The last bell rang and the Captain was slow to rise from his desk. He was concerned as we were about the situation. And then to our utter amazement TC entered the classroom! We all rose from our seats and approached him as if he was a spirit! The Captain said, "Terry, are you well enough to be here?" TC said, "I'm just a little sore." He had his right arm in a black sling. We all stepped back as he made his way towards his desk and took his seat. Bob asked, "TC, what happened?" The class gathered around his desk anxious to hear his story. TC said he was cleaning his .22 rifle early this morning before school. He had checked it and thought it was unloaded but he said he should have looked it over more carefully. He said the gun went off and the bullet hit him in the upper chest. And to our amazement he unbuttoned his white shirt and pointed to a Band-Aid on his chest and carefully pulled his shirt down over his shoulder and under the arm sling exposing a second Band-Aid on his back. As he was doing this he repeated what the doctor had told him. The bullet entered his chest, hit a rib, ricocheted to his collar bone, and exited his back causing no serious damage to any internal organs. It was wonderful that TC escaped a more serious fate and we all rejoiced that our friend was with us. TC said, "It was just in and out."

Chapter 15
First Snow

The weather was getting cooler each day and it was especially raw this Friday. The walk to school was miserable. I entered the old building and went downstairs to my locker behind the bleachers and removed my coat and stored it away. I joined Huck and James standing against the east wall of the old gym under the basketball backboard and leaned against the blue mat that hung on the wall. We watched the girls who were gathered in small groups consisting of from three to eight or more conducting their independent conversations. Huck asked James and I if we were going to town tonight and I said I planned to after the game. James said that he wasn't planning on coming back to town tonight. Tank walked over from the bleachers and pointed to some imaginary item on James' shirt under his chin and James fell for the old trick. As soon as James looked to see what Tank was pointing at, Tank raised his finger briskly and flipped James' nose to Huck's and my enjoyment. James gave Tank a courtesy smile to assure him he thought it was cool, hoping to avoid any further pranks. The first bell rang and I said, "I'll see you all tonight." Tank said, "If you're lucky!" We made our way behind the bleachers and to our lockers where we retrieved books required for our first class. Tank had Ag Class and James, Huck, and I had Business Class. I walked over to Huck who was fiddling around with something. It appeared that he didn't want any passersby to notice what he was up to. He carefully presented me a small object rolled in a brown paper hand towel. In the gloom behind the bleachers it looked like a fishing fly, but as I examined the object, I saw it had a hair pin and what appeared to be some kind of hair on the opposite end. Huck proudly announced, "These are dart flippers." "I made the tail from clumps of hair pulled out of the brushes used to clean drawings in drafting." I had made hair pin flippers before by bending a hair pin in a way that provided a good sting when bumped against someone, but it was ingenious to make an airborne flipper! Huck carefully took the dart from my hand and placed it in the paper towel with the others. He rolled the towel into a small cylindrical bundle, looked both directions, pulled up his right pant leg and inserted the darts in his sock, removed his books from his locker and off to Business Class we went.

James was already in the classroom, as well as Freeman. Huck and I took our seats one row from the back. As the rest of the class took their seats, the third and last bell rang. Mrs. Heath took a stack of papers from her desk and handed them to Terry, asking him to take one and pass them on. Before the white mimeographed papers were in our hands we could smell the scent of the chemicals that magically transferred the light blue text to each page. To our joy, it was just an exercise we were going to do in class and not a pop quiz. Our teacher instructed us to read the problem and write in a solution. We then would have a class discussion regarding our answers. Soon Huck and I were done. Neither one of us gave the problem much thought.

Our chairs were more modern than some found in other classrooms. These slightly resembled the old dark varnished wooden chairs with the initials, hearts, and various other carvings on the writing surface that wrapped around from the right side, but these chairs were a newer vintage. They were made from light colored laminated plywood with a brownish metal frame. Mrs. Heath arranged the chairs with an aisle down the center of the rows as well as each end. She would walk between the chairs and each side as she taught. Huck made eye contact with me as he slowly advanced his right hand down his trouser leg and after looking around to see if anybody was watching removed the rolled up paper towel from his sock with the darts. He folded back the towel on one end exposing the tail hair and slipped the small package inside the bottom binder ring in his notebook. He then moved the mimeographed paper down, so it was even with the notebook paper secured by the binding rings concealing the brown paper towel. Huck then focused his eyes on Freeman who was sitting three rows forward left, center of the middle aisle. Huck was sitting on the right of the center aisle. Huck looked at me as to receive approval of a possible target. It took a few seconds for me to realize what Huck was trying to say but I quickly approved by slightly nodding.

As soon as Mrs. Heath reached her desk and started the class discussion about the handout Huck began to sneak out a dart. He slowly took a dart and moved it to the underside of the writing surface holding it there with light pressure from his thumb. Huck then took a look around to see if any one noticed and carefully cocked the flipper. Assured he was in the clear, he awaited his chance. Mrs. Heath looked down and seemed to be trying to open a desk drawer. Huck held the dart, between his index finger and thumb, and threw it at Freeman hitting him in the elbow. He jerked and grabbed his arm; the dart fell under his chair. He wasn't sure what happened. Huck began to remove another dart from the brown paper towel in his notebook. He took the dart and placed it under the edge of the writing surface of the desk as he did the last one, holding it with his thumb. Christine asked Mrs. Heath a question about a problem on the handout and when the teacher walked to Christine to help her Huck threw another dart, hitting Freeman in the center of his back. Freeman received a good sting from this one too. Freeman turned around abruptly in his chair and Mrs. Heath took notice but returned to answering Christine's question, then returned to her desk. Freeman tried to reach behind him to rub the area where the dart hit him but it was like an itch that you just couldn't reach. He turned and took a long look at Huck and me. Freeman knew something was going on but he did not notice the two darts lying on the floor under his chair.

Freeman usually would wear a white shirt to school and today wasn't any different. Huck carefully removed the third dart and handed it to me. I didn't have a good shot because I was sitting just to the right of Huck although I threw the dart hitting the chair leg. Mrs. Heath sensed something was going on but wasn't sure what was happening yet. In the meantime, Freeman took his notebook and placed it behind him. The chair back had only one horizontal slat about five inches wide, connected to the brownish metal frame. The back rest was positioned about two inches above the frame so this left ample space between the wooden back rest and the chair seat. With the note book placed in the gap, Freeman lowered himself, slumping down in the chair with only his head above the chair back. Huck looked at me and I started to laugh until I heard Mrs. Heath's chair make a high pitched squeak as she pushed it back and rose. It was obvious she was on a mission! Our teacher walked straight to Freeman and said, "Harold, what are you doing?" Freeman didn't have an answer. I don't ever remember him ever being questioned about his behavior and when the opportunity arose he was speechless. Mrs. Heath stood with her hands behind her, slowly tapping the back of her right hand onto the open palm of her left. Then without notice, she grabbed Freeman by the arm and briskly raised him to standing position. The notebook fell to the floor and when it did Mrs. Heath noticed one of the darts lying beside the chair leg. She reached down to retrieve it and when she did she saw the other two darts and picked them up too. Her scorn for Freeman's unusual behavior shifted from him to Huck and me. She stepped into the center of the aisle, hands once again behind her only this time she pressed her tongue against the inside of her bottom lip and nodded her head slowly up and down. That look alone would send a shiver down the most mischievous rascal. Huck and I sat there defending ourselves the best we could with an expression of total wonderment. Mrs. Heath slowly returned to her desk at the front of the class with darts in hand, repeatedly thumping her hand clenched around the darts into her open palm of the other, behind her back. She reached her desk and opened the center drawer and placed the darts inside and closed the drawer with a slam. The bell rang and we both thought she would request us to stay behind but nothing was said. We left the class room with much anxiety, knowing her judgment was yet to come.

James asked us in the hall way, "What was that

about?" Huck said, "I don't know," with his best bewildered expression. I knew Huck thought we were in big trouble because of the way he answered James. We expected to be summoned to the principal's office but the day passed leaving us to wonder what our fate might be. Maybe she wasn't going to do anything, no, not Mrs. Heath. I knew she would have the upper hand. She always did.

I met Huck uptown that evening. He drove an old farm truck to town. It wasn't very large. It had a bed about ten feet long with four foot sides. He had parked the truck by the phone booth at the Marathon Station. We entered the Highway Café and I spoke to Diane. She hadn't been in the restaurant much longer than we had. She said she couldn't stay because her parents were picking her up at the school. I ask her if I could walk her back to the high school and she said sure. She was wearing a skirt and sweater and had her coat over her arm. I said, "It's getting cold outside, let me help you with your coat." I told Huck that I'd be back as he surveyed the crowd. Diane and I left the Highway and had a pleasant conversation as we made our way to the high school. We were just approaching the east side of the new building when she said, "There's Mom and Dad's car. Thanks for walking with me Bryan." Before I could answer she was running towards the car. She turned at the side of the car and waved before she opened the door and disappeared. I walked back towards town wishing we could have had more time together but my melancholy mood changed when it started to snow.

By the time I reached Main Street the sidewalk was already covered. The snow was coming down in large wet flakes. I saw Huck in front of the pool hall and he waved me to cross the street. Huck reached down and scooped up some snow and packed it into a snow ball, which he threw at a passing car. I stooped over and got a handful of snow and it packed well making a perfect snowball. I threw mine towards the restaurant and it landed harmlessly on the sidewalk but did bring a loud hey from a guy standing in front of the hangout. Huck said, "I've got an idea." Before I could ask what, he said, "Come on, let's get to the truck." As we hurriedly walked towards the truck, he said that I could ride in the back and throw snowballs as he drove down the street.

More and more kids were standing on the sidewalk watching the snow fall. It was a beautiful first snow of the season. I climbed into the bed of the old truck. I could hear Huck pumping the foot feed to prime the cold engine and on the third try the engine started. As Huck warmed the engine I prepared as many snowballs as time would allow laying them in a neat row on top of the truck cab. Huck pulled the truck from beside the telephone booth, across the filling station drive onto Main Street and slowly drove east. I had a hard packed snowball in my right hand and one in the left ready to transfer to my throwing arm. As we approached Hawk Eye's Pool Hall, I started my bombardment. There was a lot of yelling. It caught them by surprise. A few snowballs were hurled back but we were out of range. Huck turned left on York Street and circled the block as I replenished my ammo. As we turned onto Main Street, the yelling and jeers erupted again. Now there were more people standing on the sidewalk and many had also collected ammo. As we slowly came into range a volley of snowballs flew in both directions. I was down to my last snowball and at the end of my range too. I threw it as hard as I could, not targeting anyone in particular, just toward the group of people. The snowball caromed off the hood of an old De Soto and hit Hawk Eye. I could see the guys pointing and laughing at Hawk Eye as he cussed his way into the relative safety of the pool hall.

Huck stopped in front of Wolfs and I joined him and we crossed the street to Murphs. Huck said he was going to drink a Coke and then he would need to head for home. I said I would be heading home too, before the snow got over my shoes. The usual group was behind the cooler sitting on boxes smoking and drinking soft drinks. Bob was at the counter and had just ordered a boloney and longhorn cheese sandwich with mustard. Murph had a bad leg which he wrapped in bread sacks. He walked slowly and dragged his bad leg. He reached the meat cutter and turned, removing a tube of garlic boloney from the old cooler and placed it on the meat slicer. He laid a pre-cut piece of wax paper on the well used butcher block, opened a bread sack and placed two slices on the wax paper. Murph turned on the meet slicer and pushed the boloney toward the circular blade. The spinning blade cut the slice perfectly. Murph returned the boloney to the cooler and removed a tube of longhorn cheese, repeating the process. He picked up the cheese and boloney from the stainless steel tray and carefully placed them both on one of the bread slices. Murph picked up a well used knife, removed the lid off a mustard jar and coated the other piece of bread. He replaced the lid and wiped the knife blade with a towel that always hung from his white apron. Murph placed the mustard covered piece of bread on the stack of boloney, longhorn cheese, and bread. He folded the wax paper over, picked up the sandwich and made his way back to the counter. Murph laid the sandwich on the counter and Bob said, "Ring me up a Coke too Murph." Bob put a quarter, dime and two pennies on the counter. Murph pulled the rawhide shoe string, opening the cash register drawer and placed the coins into their respective places, then pushed the cash drawer closed with the back of his fingers.

Bob ask, "What's up fellows?" I told Bob about snow balling the guys in front of the pool hall and hitting Hawk Eye with the last one. Bob laughed and Tank came up wanting to know what was so funny. Huck told Tank over Bob's laughter. Bob caught his composure and ask, "What kind of trouble are you in over darting Freeman in Mrs. Heath's class?" Huck said, "I don't know. We haven't heard a thing."

Huck and I decided Monday morning we were not going to be reprimanded for the dart caper until we were in the Captain's class after lunch. The Captain was shuffling some papers at the podium as we noisily took our seats. He said, "Good afternoon, something has been brought to my attention. I would like to congratulate those involved in producing the flying hair pin flippers." He held up a dart and turned it side to side inspecting as he spoke. "Mrs. Heath and I are so proud of your manufacturing skills that we decided at least two of you should receive special recognition, therefore, we are sending letters to your parents. In the future please refrain from destroying our drafting plate brushes or other school property." The Captain and Mrs. Heath knew the letters to our parents would be very effective, and it was!

Two days passed and on Wednesday evening at the supper table Mom removed a folded envelope from her apron pocket and handed it to Dad. He said, "What is this?" Mom said, "Read it, it's about our oldest son's school activities." Dad read the letter and handed it back to mom. He said, "I guess you can do without the car for the next two weeks." I said, "But Dad, I've got a date with Debby Saturday!" "You better plan on walking then," Dad said.

Chapter 16
New Awareness

The Band was booked almost every Saturday night throughout the spring and summer. Johnny kept us busy learning new songs. We respected his dedication and realized the importance of promotion. Johnny's work, unnoticed by most, was the backbone of our success. During our Thursday evening practice session he had a talk with us about our future. Doug and I were going to be seniors and Johnny was concerned about the future. He gave us two options. He had spoken with a producer in Nashville about recording a record. Johnny wanted a commitment from each of us if we decided to pursue recording. He explained that he expected us to continue through next summer. The second option was to finish our booking commitments through the next school year and have our last performance sometime just before school was out for summer vacation. Johnny asked us to talk it over and said we would discuss it in the near future.

The war continued to escalate and it was almost a certainty that all males, classified 1-A, would be drafted. The alternatives were getting a student deferment by going on to college or getting married and have a child.

We heard about many people going to Canada to avoid the draft but this didn't happen in our community. The draft was one unavoidable issue facing us and if we didn't do anything Uncle Sam would. At our next practice session we unanimously decided to play until next spring and call it quits. Johnny was disappointed but he also knew reality. He brought up football this fall. He wanted to know if Doug or I intended to play. Johnny explained that he had the opportunity to book many sock hops after Friday night football games and if Doug or I decided to play he would hold off on booking Friday nights. I made the decision not to go out for the team my senior year, Doug followed. The Silhouette's played most every Friday and Saturday night throughout the summer and autumn months. I missed football and felt like I had let my buddies on the team down but thankfully they understood.

Our Industrial Arts Teacher, The Captain, accepted a teaching position elsewhere. Our new teacher was Mr. MacArthur. He had a dry personality and most of us missed the Captain. Mr. MacArthur had an annoying habit of saying thank you too much. Regardless of the circumstance, he usually would end the conversation by saying thank you.

Bob put him to the test one day by greasing the door knob. The wooden door, opening into the Industrial Arts Classroom was heavy and above it was a hydraulic door cylinder providing more resistance than required. Bob helped himself to a jar of Vaseline used in shop class for lubricating various items and applied a generous amount on the door knob. Mr. MacArthur was study hall monitor after lunch and our class was next. This gave Bob ample time to do a grease job on the knob. He held the door open with his foot while encouraging us to come into the classroom before the teacher arrived. We took our seats and soon Mr. MacArthur entered the classroom wiping his hands with his white handkerchief. He folded the handkerchief and placed it on the corner of his desk and said, "Thank you. Thank you for lubricating our door knob, although I don't think it required lubrication." We all snickered, but his response dampened the humor. That appeared to be his tactic for the year and it worked.

Before I left for school, I told Mom I would meet her at the west doors leading into the new building and cafeteria. This morning was Senior Breakfast Day. Parents joined their soon-to-graduate children for breakfast served by the cafeteria staff. Many of the parents I knew, like Tank's mother and father. Tanks mother suffered from arthritis and her hands were crippled by the disease. Letha Belle was followed closely by her twin sons and Mom and I. Les and I talked about fishing as we waited for the line to move forward. After we were all served Mr. Tucker ask Rev. Nika to pray. After breakfast we said goodbye to our parents and left the new building heading to the old and our classes.

This was the first activity leading towards graduation. It was a good breakfast and it was good to put parents' faces with fellow classmates although there seemed to be a somberness surrounding the breakfast. We were excited about graduating that spring, something we had anticipated for the last few years but it also meant leaving the protection of our classmates, and yes, teachers. It meant, for some, the first time away from home. These possibilities became closer each day and it seemed time now raced forward instead of creeping along at a snails pace.

The war and its ramifications continued to escalate as well as the nightly news coverage. By now we were all concerned. Our nation was becoming a divided society because of what was happening in South East Asia. The uncertainly gripped us all.

The Silhouette's were scheduled to play at home this weekend. It would be our last performance. It had been an exceptional opportunity to play music and meet many people at high school sock hops, prom dances, and teenage dances scattered over East Central Illinois and Western Indiana but extra special to play at our home town American Legion.

Saturday we met at the barn and instead of loading our equipment into a U-Haul, we placed the guitars, amps, and drums in our cars, or I should say borrowed parent's cars. Johnny called us together in the room where we spent many hours working out the music and lyrics of top ten songs, for our last pep talk. Johnny said with an unusual quiver in his voice, "Boys, it has been fun, always remember tonight! Now let's get up to the Legion and give them what they came to hear!" It was obvious Johnny was going to miss the weekly excitement and challenges of managing the Silhouettes.

There was a large group of people already standing on the large front porch of the Legion as we drove up. Thankfully Tank had taken it upon himself to ask people to leave four parking spaces open for us. He met us in the street as we approached and directed us into our parking spaces. He and a few other guys volunteered to help us carry in our equipment. Usually we would thank volunteers and move our equipment ourselves but tonight was special and we welcomed the help.

The crowd was overflowing onto the front porch, steps, and onto the sidewalk in front of the Legion. We could hear the footsteps above as we sat below in the kitchen area on the first floor waiting to go on stage for the last time as the Silhouettes. Just before eight o'clock

Johnny came downstairs and gave us our last minute talk as always. He was as intense as always and it was evident that he expected nothing but our best. It was reassuring to listen to Johnny tonight because of our mixed emotions but if the truth was known, I think he was more emotional than anybody. Johnny always put his all into managing and he expected no less from us. I noticed kids from adjoining towns and many I had never seen before as we took stage. As the audience started to notice us the noise subsided, and gradually the people on the dance floor turned and faced the stage. I approached the line of flood lights and started our signature song *Bull Dog* and at the same time Johnny turned on the blue lights. Steve rolled off on the drums with his intro and the dance floor turned into frenzy. Many were dancing, many clapping, and some yelling, and most noticeable, Johnny had made it to the rear of the room. He was tall, a head above most. There he was as always, with a big smile. When I made eye contact with him he gave the usual, exuberant, thumbs up!

Later, as I loaded my amp and guitar in the car, Tank asked if I was going to hang around town and I told him yes. He said, "I'll be up on the Marathon Corner." Tank had a new Plymouth two door. By the time I finished loading my equipment Tank had already joined the small fleet of cars parked on the corner filling station lot. I pulled in at the bank and walked over to Tank's car. Everyone had their radios tuned to WLS listening to Dick Biondi play the top hits. Many guys were standing outside of their cars, the volume on the radios were loud enough that it could be heard in front of the Highway Café a half block away. As cars drove past we would wolf whistle at the girls and yell insults at guys. It was customary for guys in hopped up cars to idle slowly past the Marathon several times and then suddenly accelerate and rack off between the buildings. The guys standing on the Marathon lot would then judge the loudness and performance of the car. The Highway had closed, it was 11:30. Hawk Eye was trying to empty the pool hall and most of the girls had gone home. I still needed to unload the car so I told Tank and the guys that I was going to call it a night. As I walked over to Dad's car I looked at the empty dime store and the vacated clothing store. Things were changing rapidly. I turned north on York Street and there was the usual crowd at Murphs. Bob's Ford was setting in front of the parts store. I thought about stopping but I was tired and just wanted to get home.

Monday we were to have our senior pictures taken at school so many of us brought a jacket and tie to wear. The girls were wearing nice dresses. Our photographer, Denzel, finished taking pictures by lunch time. In study hall, Mrs. Heath gave us a paper requesting information to be included in the year book under each of our pictures. She cautioned us regarding our quote. Each senior could write a short quote that will appear above the listing of club memberships, sport participation and awards, academic achievements, choir and band, just below his or her portrait. Mrs. Heath reminded us that the quotes would be subject to editing.

Next weekend our senior trip was scheduled. We were going via train to Chicago, a new experience for most of us. Class members were busy making plans. We had been warned several times by our class sponsors about the use of alcohol and cigarettes. Mrs. Heath said our luggage would be inspected if suspect. She also said, "You will be expected to stay in your assigned rooms. No room hopping!" Many of the guys were already thinking on how to smuggle vodka aboard the train.

It was rapidly becoming the season of the plastic

menace, the squirt gun. This was the one time that all class members united together, girls and guys. I have never known of anything else that brought our class together or infuriated many of our teachers like the small bright colored squirt guns. In the past they were purchased at Margie's five and ten cent store. They usually were stomped to pieces by angry teachers. Now we purchased them at Corner Hardware, due to the closing of Margies. On some days the supply didn't meet the demand. Our Principal, Mr. Tucker, and our History Teacher, Mr. Medsker, were especially ruthless in confiscating and destroying them.

In season, Mr. Medsker would set at his desk and diligently inspect us guys for any tell-tale water leakage. The small dark blue water spots that sometimes would appear around our blue-jean pockets was a dead giveaway that we were carrying a squirt gun and with only one noticed, we were all suspects.

Tank was wearing a relative new pair of blue-jeans that made any leakage more difficult to detect because they were not faded and the dark blue denim concealed the water spot although the inquisitive eye of Mr. Medsker noticed the slightest discoloration. After we had taken our seats, and the final bell rang, Mr. Medsker called Tank forward and ordered him to remove any items he had in his front pockets. Tank reluctantly removed some change from his right pocket and angrily Mr. Medsker said, "The other pocket Jerry!" Tank removed a translucent green squirt gun, a nineteen cent special and Mr. Medsker hastily grabbed for it but Tank let it drop to the floor before he could grasp it. Mr. Medsker quickly flicked the squirt gun with the toe of his polished brown wing-tip into the middle of the floor and as if almost possessed by a demon stomped the plastic squirt gun to pieces.

Red faced, Mr. Medsker ordered all the boys in the class forward, one at a time, and told us to empty our pockets. We scrambled to remove our squirt guns and hand them to the nearest girl or left them semi-hidden at our seat before we were called forward. Regardless, Mr. Medsker was able to collect at least six more guns which he pitched into the growing pile on the floor as if they were dead rats. As he finished inspecting Mike's belongings and before Mike could be seated he turned his attention to the pile of pistols. He positioned himself over the assorted multi-colored plastic guns and started to break them to small pieces by vigorously stomping on them. The longer Mr. Medsker stomped the more violent his actions become. Mr. Tucker must have heard the thud of Mr. Medsker's feet and cracking of plastic because he entered the room and assisted in the destruction. The pistol pile scattered across the floor and gave ample opportunities for both. They remotely resembled sharks in a feeding frenzy! We sat and watched the annihilation of our guns as the two stomped and grunted!

The stomping slowed to a random crush of a few scattered pieces and the principal stood aside as Mr. Medsker moved the remains towards the wall under the blackboard with the edge of his foot. Mr. Tucker looked at our history teacher briefly with a half-hearted gesture, like he wanted to speak, but left the classroom quietly. Mr. Medsker sat down at his desk looking spent. We exchanged glances at each other expressing amazement due to the two educators' violent actions. Our teacher rubbed his brow with his hand looking at the large calendar covering his desk top with black imitation leather triangles on the lower corners holding future months.

In a few minutes Mr. Medsker had regained his composure and asked us to open our text books without a word about his previous actions. Tank made a few fake coughs which helped smooth the rough edges although I wondered what was behind the intensity of our teacher and principal's actions. I wondered how something as insignificant as a toy squirt gun could invoke such apparent rage and hatred. And then, I thought about the anti-war protests held in New York, Washington, Chicago, Philadelphia, Boston, San Francisco, and other cities that entered our living rooms each night on television. How B-52's were being used for the first time against North Vietnam. What was it that separated us, the Class of 1966, from our peers? Would we be consumed with such hatred in the near future, was it something that was lying dormant within us? Time would tell. I was certain of one thing, that was the uncertainty of the future. We were about to leave a structured, protected environment into an adult world. Today, in history class, I became aware, aware that we rushing into a new arena.

Chapter 17
Chicago

The bus was scheduled to leave the high school at 11:30 Friday night taking us to Effingham where we would board our train in route to Chicago for our Senior Trip. Earlier that evening many of us guys met at the Marathon and someone had made a trip to T-Town and returned with beer. We drank openly standing beside parked cars playing music. We departed from our normal routine of yelling at passing cars trying to entice the drivers to squeal their tires or sound off their dual glass packs. Instead, we told stories of past adventures in school, reminiscing about Bob greasing the door knob, the rotten egg falling from Mr. Medsker's hat, or humming in unison in class and how upset the substitute teacher become. There was a lot of laughter and patting one another on the back for past pranks.

We broke up at about 11:00 o'clock not realizing that this was the last time we all would be assembled on the Marathon corner. Some drove their cars home and were picked up by an underclassman who took us to the horseshoe drive in front of the high school where the bus was parked. I had gone uptown with Tank, therefore he took me home and I picked up my suitcase. Mrs. Heath and several guys were standing on the sidewalk by the side of the school bus. When Tank and I approached and started to board Mrs. Heath held out her arm blocking the bus door and said, "Take your place beside the bus boys." Tank said, "What for? We didn't do anything!" "You heard me! Now stand over there and be quiet!" Mrs. Heath said as she allowed Madonna and Lynn on the bus. Just before 11:30 she faced us and said, "OK boys, I want you to open your suitcases, bags or whatever and remove any containers." Terry said, "Containers"? Mrs. Heath responded in a business like way, "Yes, all after shave bottles, mouth wash bottles, any container so I can inspect them." Well we were about to undergo the time honored tradition of Mrs. Heath's search for smuggled liquor. She walked down the line like a drill sergeant stopping to kick a bag, listening for a tell-tale clink of a glass container. She randomly chose several bottles of after shave and removed the cap taking a whiff of the contents, curling her lips and shaking her head from side to side as if questioning why anyone would desire to have such a stench drifting into the atmosphere. Passing her inspection, we were allowed to board the bus.

In less than an hour we were at the train station. The train was just about twenty minutes late. Most of us had never ridden a train. We were looking forward to the new experience. When we boarded it was like stepping back into history. The Pullman passenger car was like ones I had seen in the movies. I wondered who may have ridden in this car, surely someone famous. Our class couples snuggled together and the rest of us separated into two groups, the guys and girls. The train left Effingham ten minutes behind schedule and headed north to Chicago. I was surprised how the train rocked back and forth as it went through the night. The hypnotic swaying made it difficult to stay awake and within an hour I had fallen asleep. I awoke the first few stops the train made but became accustomed to that too.

In the gray of the early morning we entered the city and as the gray turned into early morning light, we arrived at the train station. Mrs. Heath told us to stay together and follow her. We left the train and entered Union Station's Great Hall. Mrs. Heath gathered us together between the large columns and took a head count. She told us to stay together because our bus driver would be here soon to take us to the Conrad Hilton. We stood on the pinkish marble floor waiting for the driver. Soon a black man approached wearing an Ike Jacket and cap. He briefly spoke to Mrs. Heath and turned towards us and said, "Good morning, now if you would be kind enough to follow me to the bus, I will take you to your hotel." We followed the driver across the large room and boarded the charter bus. He skillfully drove the large bus through the busy morning traffic as we marveled at the large glistening buildings in the morning sunlight. Soon our driver pulled over and stopped. The bus was equipped with a sound system. He picked up the microphone and blew into it to make sure it was working and said, "720 South Michigan Avenue, we are at your hotel, the Conrad Hilton. I will be your bus driver for the next few days and my name is Jim. Please do not leave anything on the bus as you get off and I will be back here at ten o'clock to take you to the Science and Industry Museum." We went into the lobby of the hotel and waited for Mrs. Heath to check us in at the desk. We already knew our roommates for the night. This was decided a few weeks ago.

I, as well as TC, Harvey and Terry needed to use the restroom so we hoped it wouldn't take Mrs. Heath too long. Mrs. Heath returned to our group with several envelopes with names written on them. She told us our rooms were all on the sixth floor and said whoever took the room key would be responsible for the key, room, and our roommates. We would be told when and where to meet and it was mandatory to be on time. As she called off our names, one from each group went to her and before she gave them the room key from the envelope, she circled the name of the person taking the key with a red pencil. After the room keys were passed out, she folded all the empty envelopes and put them in her large purse. Mrs. Heath then announced, "You must meet me here at ten to ten. Remember to be on time! Now you are free to take an elevator up to the sixth floor and locate your rooms." Our group, TC, Terry, Harvey and I rushed toward one of the many elevators in the large lobby. We rode up and found our room, 612 and waited our turn in the bathroom.

At nine twenty we left the room and rode the elevator back down to the lobby. Christine and her group were the only others waiting. Soon others exited the elevators and joined us along with Jim, our bus driver. Just before ten Mrs. Heath stepped from an elevator and walked over to us standing near the main doors. She removed a paper and called each one of our names and we responded, "Here" or some guys said "Yep", the latter receiving a glance over the top of her eye glasses. Satisfied that we were all present she told Jim, "I think we are ready." Jim said, "OK, please follow me." We left the hotel and boarded the bus. Jim skillfully maneuvered the bus through the traffic and soon we were in a parking lot in front of the Science and Industry Museum. Jim picked up the microphone and announced that we should be back at two o'clock and that a restaurant or snack bars could be located on the lower floor. Mrs. Heath asked Jim to announce that we were to wait on the sidewalk and we would be given our entry tickets as soon as she returned. We walked up the steps and waited in front of the massive building. Soon she returned with our tickets. She reminded us again of our time schedule as she handed us our tickets.

As we entered, we saw a stuffed elephant standing on a small knoll in the lobby surrounded by a red velvet rope suspended by brass posts. Several of us guys approached the elephant and joined other visitors looking at the exhibit. I looked at Larry and gave him the secret signal to do his thing. I pulled my ear lobe and Larry started his act. He made eye contact with a young boy standing next to his father and sniffed the air and made an audible moan contorting his face. The young boy reached for his father's hand and Larry jumped over the red velvet rope and turned looking at the young boy, moaned and snorted again taking the posture of a chimpanzee. The father led his frightened son away and Larry quickly returned to the spectator side of the red rope. We all hurried away in the opposite direction the father and son went, laughing until our sides hurt. Soon the grandeur of the museum replaced our desire to make fools of ourselves and we enjoyed a fast paced exploration of the Science and Industry Museum. I wish we would have had more time; in fact, we never stopped to eat a snack. We all met back at the bus at precisely two o'clock and there waiting on us was Jim and Mrs. Heath. Our teacher once again called off our names and we boarded the bus for the short ride to the Prudential Building. We saw sea gulls flying in the brisk wind and sail boats moored along Lake Shore Drive, and there it was, the tall building that we were scheduled to visit. Jim halted the bus at the bus stop and asked that we quickly disembark because he wasn't to park in the city bus zone. He also asked us to be sure we had our personal belongings with us. We stepped out of the bus and Mrs. Heath ordered us to stay in our group when we entered the building. I looked up at the tall building. We entered the lobby and again waited as Mrs. Heath confirmed our arrangements with the receptionist. She handed out our passes to enter the observation deck and we boarded the elevator in small groups and made the forty-one floor accent. We stepped out of the elevator into a small lobby that contained a gift shop. We didn't take the time to go into the shop but presented our passes to the attendant standing beside the double doors opening to the observation deck. The view was spectacular. There were telescopes mounted around the observation deck. They had a mechanism that resembled the coin slots on a parking meter. You needed to insert a quarter into the base of the telescope mount and turn a small handle, no doubt something connected to a timer which allowed you ten minutes of viewing. None of us guys looked through the telescope but Donna and Janice were using one. We spent little less than an hour on the observation deck. Harvey, Swish, Terry, and I checked out the gift shop. We were getting real hungry and could smell an aroma that only made us more so. Inside we found a snack bar. Swish, Terry and I purchased a hot dog and Coke. Harvey purchased himself a tuna sandwich and Coke. There were circular tables mounted high on chrome pedestals placed around a small room and against one wall were condiments consisting of mustard, ketchup, relish and onions. We fixed up our sandwiches and wolfed them down standing at one of the small tables. Harvey was the last one to finish. We took the elevator down to the lobby and waited for everybody to gather. Mrs. Heath took another head count before we left the building and boarded the bus for our return trip to the Conrad Hilton.

Jim gave Mrs. Heath the microphone and she announced that we would walk as a group to the Blackstone Theater. She said to meet at seven in the lobby. We went to our rooms and TC said he was going to rest. Terry and I decided to investigate the hotel and look for a place to eat. Harvey said he was going to look up Gary.

We gathered in the lobby and when Mrs. Heath was satisfied we all were present, we walked the short distance to the Blackstone Theater. I was surprised when we were ushered to our seats. It was the first time that any of us had been to a professional theater performance. The play was *The Odd Couple*. The performance was captivating. After the play we walked back to the hotel. We met Mrs. Heath and Jim in the lobby at eleven o'clock to transport us to the pier to board an excursion boat for a late night cruise on the river and lake. We all gathered and Mrs. Heath did her thing. After the head count we boarded the bus and Jim took us to the pier. We boarded the boat which had an enclosed seating area with large windows and a walkway on the deck outside. Almost everybody decided to stay inside because of the cool wind off the lake but Larry, Terry and I walked to the bow of the boat. It was great fun.

On the way back to the Conrad Hilton we noticed the blue flashing lights of a police car and a large group of young people carrying signs. They were protesting the war. Neither I nor anybody in our room had the television turned on; therefore the nightly reports of our nation's unrest with the war in Southeast Asia were vague memories until we saw the people protesting in the street. There was much we were sheltered from living in a rural area.

Jim returned us to the hotel. We were exhausted; it had been a long day. It wasn't long before we were asleep.

The next morning, we packed our belongings and met in the lobby while Mrs. Heath collected the room keys and conducted business with the front desk person. She returned, and we followed her and Jim to the bus and left the hotel for the last time in route to the train station.

It was an uneventful ride home, everyone was exhausted. Many slept on the way south. We arrived in Effingham that evening and boarded the school bus for the ride home. During the ride home I thought about the things and people I had seen in the city. It was almost too much to comprehend in a short weekend and I wanted to retain all that was possible. I wanted to remember the hum of the city, the smells, and the never ending movement of people in a hurry to reach their destination. The architecture of new and old rising up from the lake shore together in unity, unity so urgently needed during a time when circumstances and policies eroded people's ability to understand one another.

Chapter 18
Graduation

Thank goodness merchants had sold out of squirt guns. Mr. Medsker had bruised his right heal from destroying them and I wonder if he could of stayed ahead of the game, in his condition. The last week of school, I never thought the day would come. With graduation this Friday, the thought of leaving the confines of MCHS was frightening, which was strange, because of all the wishing for freedom in the past. Tomorrow we would take our final tests. Not too many were overly concerned because at this point either you knew it or you didn't. Today we were to go to Mrs. Heath's classroom and pick up our graduation gowns and hats.

We completed our final tests and the rest of the day was lackluster. I guess we were wondering about graduation. It was bittersweet, knowing that our class of fifty-three would soon graduate and each would go their separate way. Some on to college, some to jobs, some would wed their sweethearts, and some would serve their country. Tank and I had decided to go to Kansas City to school. We actually didn't know that we both had selected the same school until a few days after we were accepted.

It was good to know we would be going together and we made tentative plans about sharing an apartment.

Wednesday, we met in the new gym after lunch for graduation practice. We were not too excited about practicing although Larry said he would do his thing and Tank encouraged him. We had abbreviated classes today because all we need to do was turn in our text books. Mr. Toping asked us what our future plans were and most of the girls answered, only a few boys did. Mr. Murphy cleaned the biology room and emptied all the aquariums, terrariums, cages, and jars. The English Classroom's blackboard was spotless. It was the first time I believe I had ever seen it that way. Mrs. Kile treated us like her children today. She showed a side of herself that we instinctively knew was there, but never had seen before. Surprisingly, most of us ate lunch in the school cafeteria. We had sloppy-joes, a half peach, two carrot sticks, and cottage cheese. There wasn't anything special about our last lunch in the school cafeteria.

The girls, at least the freshman, sophomores, and juniors were dancing in the old gym after lunch. Many of the senior girls were grouped in small groups either standing close to the stage or sitting on the bleachers. Montgomery and Trish, Huck and Ginny, Terry and Barb, and TC and Phyllis were sitting on the bleachers close to the top row where they could hold hands with less of a chance of getting caught. A few guys were in the student parking lot sneaking a smoke and Tank and I were leaning against the blue pad hanging on the wall under the basketball backboard surveying the girls, commenting about certain ones once in a while. Tank asked me what I was going to do tomorrow. There wasn't any school Thursday. I really hadn't thought about it. I guess we were all thinking about Friday night. I told Tank that

I was not planning on anything particular, and the bell rang. We had been instructed to assemble in the new gym after lunch. It was strange but it seemed that many of us were reluctant to leave the old gym. The memories were rich within that well-used, yellowish colored tile floor, battleship gray bleachers, and white plastered walls. Proms, sock hops, Sadie Hawkins dances, JV basketball games, plays, school assemblies, band concerts, Villager concerts, award ceremonies, courtships, fights, pranks, and the first time the Silhouettes performed were memories now. As we left the old gym and climbed the stairs I realized that was in the past, and I think many classmates shared the same thoughts.

The new gym smelled like an old musty tent. The janitors had a tarp spread over the floor to protect it during the graduation ceremony. They were moving folding chairs from the cafeteria and band room and had already started setting them across the floor in front of a portable platform where school officials and school board members would sit. There was a podium placed along the center edge. The custodians placed chairs on each side of the small stage. In front of the lesser quantity were the three tiered steps the Villagers stood on when performing. The greater numbers of chairs were for us. There was a piano close to the three tiered steps. We slowly entered the new gym and sat on the south end of the bleachers. Mrs. Heath was having a conversation with Mr. Tucker in front of the stage and Tank gave one of his famous fake coughs, trailing it with the word, the mother of all profanity, partially disguised within the cough and subsequent throat clearing. Mr. Tucker turned to face us as well as Mrs. Heath. It was obvious Mr. Tucker was very angry, but before he could gather his thoughts, Mrs. Heath spoke, "Jerry, you haven't graduated yet, so I'd advise you to be quiet." She then calmly placed her hand on Mr. Tucker's elbow, slightly turning him away from us and continued her conversation. She was a craftsperson in controlling situations and she performed excellently today!

After several more minutes she walked toward us and said, "You will be paired with the person that you will walk in with. I'll read who the pairs will be." She read off the names to a few moans of discontentment over the pairings. She then said that we would assemble in the band room and put our robes and caps on and line up in our assigned order. We would walk in the gymnasium two by two to *Pomp and Circumstance*, using a hesitation step which she demonstrated to more moans and sighs. "Now I want you to go to the band room and pair up with your designated partner and we'll practice walking in and taking our seats," Mrs. Heath said. Tank, to everyone's enjoyment, used his personal rendition of the hesitation step as we walked toward the band room until he noticed Mr. Tucker glaring at him, then he shifted into an exaggerated march. I wasn't sure how much more Mr. Tucker would take but fortunately he was called away, I suspect just in the nick of time. We ran through the exercise another time and Mrs. Heath seemed pleased at our performance. She then said we would be called forward and presented our diplomas. She instructed us to take the diploma in our left and shake the school board member's hand. She asked Janice to come forward to help in a demonstration and after they went through the handshake and passing Mrs. Heath's papers as if they were her diploma she turned towards us and said, "There will be no comments or applauding by any of you during graduation." Then she asked, "Are there any questions?" No one was brave enough to ask anything so she said, "If not, then I will see you Friday night in the band room no later than six forty-five."

Thursday morning I went across the street and Gaiter wasn't up yet. It seemed strange to be home on a Thursday. Tomorrow we would return to school to get our report cards and be dismissed soon afterwards, then graduation that evening. I just wished it was over. I walked back across the street and Billy came out. He was going to shoot some baskets in his back yard. His granddad built him and his brothers a very nice place to play basketball, a concrete pad with a goal at one end. Billy asked if I would like to join him but I decided to go back home for a while and check on Gaiter a little later. Anson was in the back yard playing in the dirt with a toy bulldozer, busy moving imaginary yards of dirt. He was totally consumed by his construction project because he never noticed me as I walked past. I looked at my bicycle leaning against the garage. It was in a position that water would run off the roof onto it. I hadn't ridden it for some time and I noticed the water had caused the chain to rust. I thought how priorities change because last year the chain would not have had the chance to rust due to constant usage. Now, there it sat, against the garage rusting with blades of grass reaching for the sun between the spokes of its wheels. I decided to go back to Gaiters and wait for him to come out. Just as I reached the ditch in front of the house the fire whistle sounded. It seemed everything else became silent. People were listening to the fire engine's sirens, trying to detect where they were headed. In a few minutes I heard the scream of the red trucks and it sounded like they were going east. I listened until they subsided into the normal hum of a small town mixed with the occasional chirp of sparrows and a dog howling in the far distance.

Gaiter was sitting on the top of a picnic table in his back yard and I joined him. He was facing one direction with his feet resting on the board seat and I sat down on the table top facing the opposite direction. We just sat there for a long time, neither one speaking. After some time Gaiter said, "What are you going to do today?" I said, "I don't know, you got any ideas?" Gaiter didn't answer; he sat there, his fists clenched and thumbs placed on his neck, his elbows resting on his knees with the weight of his head. He often assumed this pose and sometimes would spend long periods in deep contemplation not responding to one's inquiries. After a few minutes Gaiter said, "They are talking about sending me to a school over by St. Louis this summer." I quickly responded, "Who's they?" He said, "My Grandma and Mom." He then walked over to the barn. I followed him and he pointed to a Maytag engine, a gasoline washer engine with a kick start lever. "Let's take this to the picnic table and see if it will run," Gaiter said pointing at the motor. I helped him carry the motor to the picnic table and we sat it on the board seat below the top of the table. Gaiter jostled the Maytag motor from side to side to align one of its mounting holes with a hole already in the board seat. Once aligned, he returned to the barn and found a stove bolt. He dropped the stove bolt through the hole in the motor mounting flange and table seat. No nut was used to secure the bolt but Gaiter pulled a small c-clamp from his hip pocket and clamped the opposite mounting flange to the seat. He sat on the table top again and placed his foot on the kick starter. He pumped the kick starter lever about four times and said it seemed to have good compression. I followed him back to the barn and he found an old mason jar and blew the dust out of it. Gaiter sat it outside on the sidewalk and walked back inside the barn returning with a small gasoline can and a quart can of oil. As careful as a chemist, Gaiter poured gas in the jar, then some oil. He then picked up the green tinted jar and swirled the contents holding it up to the morning sun. "Looks like it needs more gas," Gaiter said, after a careful inspection. He sat the jar down and added some and once again swirled the Mason jar inspecting his mix in the light. Gaiter, satisfied with his mixture, returned to the old Maytag and sat the jar down, mumbled something and returned to the barn. I remained at the table. Gaiter soon returned with a rusty pair of pliers and removed the fuel tank cap on the engine. He took the jar and dumped the gas into the tank with an equal amount on the picnic table seat and ground below. Gaiter replaced the cap on the tank and took a seat on the table top again. He sat there, again resting his head upon his thumbs and fists with his elbows upon his knees. I ask, "Gaiter, aren't you going to try and start it?" "Yah, just as soon as that gas dries up that is on the seat and motor." I nodded and said, "Makes good sense." We waited and soon the morning sun dried the seat and motor. Gaiter climbed down from the top of the picnic table and checked the c-clamp making sure it was tight and just as quickly returned to the table top placing his foot on the kick starter. He pressed the kick lever down and again. On the third kick the old motor came to life belching a cloud of white smoke. Gaiter quickly climbed to the ground and adjusted the carburetor settings and soon the old motor was running like a new one although the c-clamp vibrated loose and fell to the ground. When this happened, Gaiter shut off the motor and said, "I knew it would run!" I knew if Gaiter set his mind to it, he could resurrect the old washing machine motor and he did.

It soon was time for lunch so I left Gaiters and crossed Washington Street. I saw Billy still shooting baskets and walked behind his house. I ask him, "Did you hear where the fire was?" Billy said, "I think it was just east of town, someone named Ben was burning trash and got a field on fire." "The old guy who drives the tractor to town?" I ask. Billy said, "Yah, that's the one." I cut across Doc Moore's back yard and entered the back door of my house asking rather loudly, "Lunch ready?"

Tank came after lunch and asked me if I wanted to ride around and we drove the loop from Main Street down York to Cronk's IGA and back up town many times. It was a quiet Thursday afternoon so we stopped at Hawk Eye's Pool Hall and played two games of eight ball. We soon decided to drive the loop again just to make sure anybody else wasn't cruising. Tank made two laps and said nothing was going on so he was going to drop me off and go home. He pulled his green Plymouth into our drive and I said, "I'll see you tonight at graduation." Tank said, "If you are lucky!"

Hoss's Senior picture

I got to the school early and was hanging around the outside of the band room. Soon others began pulling into the student parking lot and some were also dropped off. The girls entered the band room as soon as they saw the group of guys congregated outside. Someone asked what time it was and another answered it was fifteen till and we walked into the room where most of the girls already had their graduation gowns on and were busy adjusting their hats. The guys dressed quickly, and the girls were pleased to help us adjust our blue and white tassels attached to the top of our hats. Mrs. Heath picked up a drum stick and tapped it against a music stand asking for our attention. It became quiet in the band room and she asked, "I presume you remember the order to line up?" She looked at us with an unfamiliar look, a look neither I nor my classmates had seen before. She was pleasantly smiling with a look of pride! Quickly she took a deep breath and asked, "Does anybody have any questions?" I think most of us were so amazed that she revealed a side, a side we never expected, that we were speechless! The moment disappeared as quickly as it came with the first notes of *Pomp and Circumstance.*

We quickly found our partner or our partner found us and took our places in line. Mrs. Heath, with her hand holding the door knob, of the door leading into the new gymnasium, gave one last word of instruction, "Walk slowly," and smiled again opening the door. Using the newly acquired hesitation step we entered the gymnasium, two by two and nervously made our way down the isle between people on the left and right of our procession. The gym was warm and the graduation gowns only made it warmer. The room smelled of tarpaulin and flowers. The tarp laid on the floor to protect the basketball court, and the flowers were arranged on the raised platform to the left and right of the podium. We took our seats, folding chairs left of the platform and the pianist concluded. A hush drifted over the assembled family, guests, teachers, administrators, and students like a morning fog drifting over a meadow only to be interrupted by a cough from someone in the crowd. Rev. Nika stood, approached the podium, and opened with prayer. The Villagers directed by Mr. Stewart were to the right of the platform and as soon as Rev. Nika returned to his seat the pianist played the intro and the Villagers sang *America the Beautiful*.

The reverberation of the Villagers voices still lingered in the gymnasium as Mr. Tucker approached the podium. Our principal thanked the audience for attending the graduation ceremony of the Class of 1966. He asked Mr. Stewart and the Villagers to perform another song. They sang *Moon River* and were given a robust applause. Mr. Tucker approached the podium again and introduced our Superintendent, Mr. Winlet. Mr. Tucker shook Mr. Winlet's hand as the superintendant approached the speaker's podium. The Superintendent thanked Mr. Tucker and made a short speech.

As the graduation ceremony moved forward I was overcome with a placid yet anxious feeling. It was difficult to put in words. I knew many of my classmates were experiencing the same emotion. They were physically present but their eyes contained a look that was unique to the overly warm evening. We were becoming aware that we were crossing a threshold that evening, that from this day on, most of our future was our choice. Yes, our parents would still offer advice and encourage us to make the correct choices but those choices became our choices that night.

The moment came to receive our diplomas and as Mrs. Heath instructed, we approached the school officials when our name was called and were presented our diplomas by the school board president. It was somber, yet some of the responses from family members seated before us eased the tension, and we exchanged smiles with our robed classmates. The last student, Sandra Zachery accepted her diploma and returned to her place as we all remained standing. Rev. Nika approached the podium and closed the graduation service with a benediction and the Class of 1966 returned to the band room two by two as the pianist played.

We removed our blue and white robes and placed them on a folding table as Mrs. Heath assisted in the removal of the cap tassel. We made small talk waiting on someone or something to occur but the finality of the evening weighed upon us and we quietly left the band room, some to be greeted by their parents and family waiting in the gym and a few exiting the door into the student parking lot.

Chapter 19
Water Under the Bridge

It has been said many times, but truly, it was just like yesterday when we enjoyed lazy summer afternoons swimming at the lake, or when I smell chocolate, I see the glass and chrome display case at Margie's Five and Ten. Those times are but a fond memory now. The shops and stores lining the one block of Main Street, now called Cumberland Street are gone as well as some of our classmates. Time took the Highway Café, Wal-Mart took the Corner Hardware, Vietnam took James, and an auto accident took Tank. Old age took Murph. Disease took Mark and Ann. Jerry and Gary took themselves.

We have had several class reunions in the years that followed graduation. They have been a help marking certain fads such as the disco era. Leisure suits made their appearance and short skirts as well. The first reunions gave an opportunity for many to boast of their accomplishments. This seemed to be the agenda, but as years passed, things have changed. Now there seems to be no agenda. We join together every five years, the Class of 1966, for the simple joy of being together again. Now the discussion revolves around grandkids, retirement and the joy of being united again.

Yes, a lot of water has gone under the bridge but let us not forget those glorious days of childhood. Those days filled with anticipation and wonderment. Time has passed, much water was gone under the bridge but we can always remember when....